D0065371

More Advance Praise for
I've Seen a Lot of Famous People Naked, and They've Got Nothing on You!

"Jake Steinfeld is proof to all of us that we really can make our professional goals and dreams realities without compromising who we are. This book is a reflection of Jake himself—empowering, motivating, and inspiring. If there were such a thing as an MBA in street smarts or common sense, this book would be required reading."
　　—Steve Netzley
　　　Founder and President, Euro RSCG DRTV

"Jake embodies all the vital talents of a successful entrepreneur—honesty, enthusiasm, sincerity, passion for customer satisfaction, leadership, and fitness market expertise—coupled with a relentless determination to be successful. He's a business force that can't be denied."
　　—Warren V. "Pete" Musser
　　　Founder and Chairman Emeritus
　　　Safeguard Scientifics, Inc.

"Jake's positive energy and passion have inspired many people to reach their goals."
　　—Peter Morton
　　　Founder and Chairman, Hard Rock Hotel & Casino, Las Vegas

I've seen a lot of famous people naked,

and they've got nothing on you!

I've seen a lot of famous people naked,

and they've got nothing on you!

BUSINESS SECRETS FROM THE ULTIMATE STREET-SMART ENTREPRENEUR

JAKE STEINFELD

FOREWORD BY STEVEN SPIELBERG

AMACOM AMERICAN MANAGEMENT ASSOCIATION
NEW YORK • ATLANTA • BRUSSELS • CHICAGO • MEXICO CITY • SAN FRANCISCO
SHANGHAI • TOKYO • TORONTO • WASHINGTON, D.C.

Special discounts on bulk quantities of AMACOM books are available to corporations, professional associations, and other organizations. For details, contact Special Sales Department, AMACOM, a division of American Management Association, 1601 Broadway, New York, NY 10019.
Tel.: 212-903-8316. Fax: 212-903-8083.
Web site: www.amacombooks.org

This publication is designed to provide accurate and authoritative information in regard to the subject matter covered. It is sold with the understanding that the publisher is not engaged in rendering legal, accounting, or other professional service. If legal advice or other expert assistance is required, the services of a competent professional person should be sought.

Body By Jake Total Body Trainer is a trademark of Body By Jake Enterprises, LLC. Ab Scissor and Cardio Cruiser are trademarks of Body By Jake Global, LLC.

Library of Congress Cataloging-in-Publication Data

Steinfeld, Jake.
I've seen a lot of famous people naked, and they've got nothing on you! : business secrets from the ultimate street-smart entrepreneur / Jake Steinfeld ; foreword by Steven Spielberg.
p.   cm.
Includes index.
ISBN 0-8144-0860-5
1. New business enterprises.   2. Success in business.   3. Body By Jake Enterprises.   I. Title.

HD62.5.S7416   2006
658.4'21—dc22   2005007100

© 2006 Body By Jake Global LLC
All rights reserved.
Printed in the United States of America.

This publication may not be reproduced,
stored in a retrieval system,
or transmitted in whole or in part,
in any form or by any means, electronic,
mechanical, photocopying, recording, or otherwise,
without the prior written permission of AMACOM,
a division of American Management Association,
1601 Broadway, New York, NY 10019.

Printing Number

10   9   8   7   6   5   4   3   2   1

Every morning I wake up wanting to be better than the day before. I have that drive because of you . . . my family!

This book, then, is dedicated to my wife Tracey, my daughter Morgan, and my three boys Nick, Zach, and Luke.

contents

foreword

Jake Steinfeld's presence in my life is a gift, and I mean that literally.

I first met him in 1982 when a friend gave me one session with a personal trainer as a birthday present. I must admit I had my reservations about this supposed gift. For starters, the mere idea of inviting someone over to the house to criticize my physique didn't sound the least bit appealing. I was also convinced the gift was actually retribution for some horrible indiscretion I had once committed against my friend, but one I could no longer recall. Still, it was the early eighties, and the personal fitness era was well under way. Also, I needed the help more than I cared to admit. I figured it was worth at least a meeting with this guy Jake, so I gave him a call.

Jake's infectious enthusiasm and boundless energy were already evident when I greeted him at the door. I was prepared for a Muscle Beach monster, but found instead a lovable Long Islander with a voice that sounded like a bass drum being played over a loudspeaker. He gave me the nickname Spiels in that first meeting, and to this day I still laugh when someone tells me there's a man on the phone asking for Wiels, the name that Jake finally picked for me.

Those first few workout sessions were a struggle, but I am proud to say I am one of the few who have been through a Jake Steinfeld workout and not been visited by the puke monster. He was an excellent physical trainer—supportive without being abusive, and critical without being condescending. He helped me get over my fear of heavy, menacing objects—i.e. free weights—and I regaled him with stories from the trenches of Tinseltown.

We got to be good friends. He showed me the proper technique for using the bench press, and I showed him important things, like how to eat caviar with a spoon. The stories from those early days are memorable and too numerous to mention here, but I will say the sight of Jake battling seasickness aboard a deep-sea fishing boat is an image I will not soon forget.

Over the course of our travels I also introduced him to my friends, some of whom joined his ever-growing list of clientele. He eventually became the premiere physical trainer in Hollywood, and I asked Jake if he ever considered opening his own company. He told me he thought about it all the time, but had reservations about his ability to succeed in the business world. In Jake's mind, entrepreneurs were well-educated people with MBAs, not regular guys without a college education. At the time I wasn't a college graduate either, and I pointed this out to him. Without believing in myself when no one else did, I reasoned, I would never have gotten anywhere either.

Jake has often cited his relationship with me as a source of inspiration in the early part of his career, but I was only doing for him what he had done for me in our workouts. He made me believe I could accomplish something I was convinced was impossible, and it wasn't long before Jake's confidence in his own entrepreneurial skills started to take off.

He was building his business on another strength—a love of people—and he infuses this love into everyone he meets. He makes you feel good about yourself mentally as well as physically, and makes you view the world for the beautiful place it is. More than twenty years later Jake is still my living proof that street smarts and believing in oneself are the keys to succeeding at anything in life, and I am proud of him for deciding to share his sage advice through the book you are holding. He may have come into my life as just a birthday gift, but he remains in it as the greatest gift of all— a friend.

Steven Spielberg

acknowledgments

A true street-smart entrepreneur puts together a team of talented profession-als to help him build on his strengths, and I've had the benefit of a top-notch group on this book project, starting with my literary agent Jan Miller, my AMACOM executive editor Jacquie Flynn, and AMACOM president and publisher Hank Kennedy. I'd also like to thank Ed Reilly, president and CEO of the American Management Association, for his support.

For their special contributions and expertise, I'd also like to thank Lion's Gate Entertainment CEO Jon Feltheimer, and Kevin Beggs, president of pro-gramming and production at Lion's Gate.

Finally, there is my team in the trenches: my *Body By Jake* gang, and writer Wes (Minster) Smith, the wordsmith for this project from start to finish.

I've seen a lot of **famous people naked,** and **they've got nothing on you!**

the naked truth

I DON'T KNOW how she tracked down my telephone number because I never got around to having it listed. But this was one message I couldn't ignore.

"Jake, I heard about what you've been doing for other actresses around town and I want to talk to you about your services—for me and for a very close friend of mine too!"

You gotta love Hollywood. There I was back in the early 1980s, a regular guy from Baldwin, Long Island, who had stumbled into this incredible sideline that had me sweatin' with stars like Priscilla Presley, Harrison Ford, and Bette Midler.

My client list was growing every day with calls from the most beautiful and talented people in the entertainment industry, not to mention many of the most powerful producers and directors.

It was heady stuff. I had no idea where it was going in those early days, but I was enjoying the ride. It was crazy because every day was such a wild adventure. I'd retired from Cortland State in cold, cold upstate New York after freezing my kneecaps off on the lacrosse field. I'd headed for Los

Angeles as a teenage bodybuilder with dreams of becoming Mr. America. But I'd dropped out of that too after seeing what you had to take to compete. Steroids weren't illegal then, but I wanted nothing to do with them. I never saw how they fit in with the whole concept of building a healthy body. I preferred to do my bodybuilding the natural way, but that meant I'd never be able to compete for the big titles back then.

As it turned out, staying natural and going with my gut took me in a whole new world. Without even realizing what I was getting into, I created an entire industry when I became the first personal fitness trainer to the stars. Before I knew it, I was in business.

Me? In business? You better believe it.

It started with a young actress who lived in my apartment complex in Studio City. She needed to tighten up for a bit part in a commercial that called for her to wear a bikini. Word got around that I'd whipped her into shape and suddenly I was getting all sorts of interesting calls.

Like that message on my machine.

"Jake," she cooed, "I really want to give you to my friend as a birthday present!"

She gave me an address in Coldwater Canyon. It was a neighborhood of hot properties. The bold and the beautiful. The young and the restless. All on their way to becoming the rich and the famous.

Needless to say, I showed up at the appointed hour ready to rock.

It was a swank place with swell views, like something out of a Hollywood movie. And I felt like the star of the movie.

I rang the bell as the music from the movie score played out in my head.

A gorgeous woman answered the door. Perfect!

"I'm Cathy," she said. "My friend is excited and waiting to unwrap my present!"

She led me through the big, open house. It smelled like California tanning oil. Soft jazz was playing on a stereo.

We entered a room at the end of a long, dark hallway, so when we turned the corner it took a few seconds for my eyes to adjust to the light streaming in from the big glass windows overlooking the pool and the valley below.

Then, what to my wondering eyes should appear but . . .

The naked Spielberg!

"Hi, Jake," he said. "I'm Steven."

Gotcha!

Come on now! You can't *still* be thinking that ol' Jake is going to write about seeing famous people naked.

Well, once again, let me set the record straight. I did see a lot of famous people naked but not in the buff, unclothed, *nekkid*, naked. Instead, I saw them stripped of the trappings of fame and fortune. No entourages. No public relations flaks. No makeup. No Gucci. No Armani. No bull.

That particular day, I met Steven Spielberg in the raw. I saw him as he really is: A regular guy. Just like all those other celebrities you read about and watch on the big screen. They are all regular people with extraordinary beauty, brains, talent, and drive, as well as the usual insecurities, neuroses, warts, pimples, and hangnails that we all have. In other words, like the title says: They got nothin' on you!

At our first meeting, there was nothing flashy about Steven Spielberg. He seemed to be a real regular guy: skinny, with glasses, wearing a T-shirt, gym shorts, black socks, and tennis shoes. He was friendly but very nervous, because, as he said, "I haven't exercised since the eighth grade."

E.T. had bigger biceps.

"Please don't hurt me," he said.

He was joking, but it took a while to get him to relax and understand that I was there to help him get healthier, not browbeat him like a drill sergeant. He was feeling vulnerable and a little intimidated, so we just worked with my low-key gear—a towel, a broomstick, and a chair—to do some basic stuff. He got through it all and actually did very well. I could tell that he was not a guy who quit easily even though physical exercise was not his natural thing.

I thought it had gone great for our first session, though he was sweating like a Miami roofer at the end of it. I told him to drink some water and walk around a while. I had to get going to my next scheduled appointment with Bette Midler, who lived a few miles away. Bette was still getting ready for the workout when I got to her house, so I called my apartment to check my answering machine. There were five calls—all of them from Spielberg.

"Jake, I can't move my arms."

"Jake, now my legs are numb . . . is this normal?"

"Jake, I'm really getting worried. I can't move my neck; I think I'm partially paralyzed. Does this happen to everyone? Call me!"

I got him on the phone before he called 911 for a Med-Evac chopper.

"I thought I was supposed to feel better after your visit," Spielberg said.

"Spiels [I'd already given him his first official *Body By Jake* nickname], take it easy," I told him. "Drink some water, do some stretches, and we'll work out the kinks in tomorrow's session."

Cathy, his girlfriend, called me that night. When I heard her voice, I was afraid she was going to tell me that he had decided to call off the one-week trial. Or that he'd checked into workout rehab.

"He loves it!" she said instead. "He wants you to come to his beach house and keep it going next week too."

We talked constantly during his workouts. *Jaws* had been his first huge commercial success and he was still shocked and thrilled to be in a position where he no longer had to worry about paying the bills. I was still very much in the bill-paying position, so I wanted to know how it felt. Listening to him made success seem much more accessible to me. He wasn't cocky about it. He didn't lord it over me. He was trying to get a handle on the fact that people not only understood and enjoyed his movies; they were throwing huge sums of money at him to get him to make more of them.

Spiels still saw himself as the smart kid from Cincinnati who had trouble fitting in when his family moved to Arizona and then California. It had only been a few years since he'd been turned down by both the UCLA and USC film schools. Even if no one else remembered his struggles, he never forgot that he had to sneak onto the lots of the studios in Hollywood where he begged and bothered executives until they let him make movies.

In some ways, I think he still felt like a guy who'd snuck into the grownups' party, or at least like a kid who'd been caught up on a fantasy ride based on his wildest dreams. I wasn't riding as high but I often had the same feeling in those days. That's another reason we hit it off: We felt like a couple of regular guys who'd hitched a ride on the Hollywood express.

The next thing I knew, I was flying on the Warner Brothers jet with him to meetings, or jumping on the Concorde to check out locations across the world. I traveled abroad for the first time with him. My nickname for him eventually became "Wiels" because the wheels in his brain were always churning up new things, just little ideas like *Jaws* and *Indiana Jones*. He also introduced me to caviar, five-star hotels, and to success and achievement at levels that neither one of us "regular guys" could have dreamed in our younger days.

I watched and learned as my friend reinvented himself and his life. He didn't just help me think big, he helped me see that life offers limitless possibilities and opportunities. Hanging out with him, I lived it too. I experienced the tastes, smells, sound and feel of the good life. It was like sampling the world's healthiest addictive drug: success.

I was hooked and Wiels was my source, my supplier. I'd seen him stripped down to gym shorts and a t-shirt so I knew that he was a regular guy. Sure he's brilliant and talented, but like the rest of us, he struggled until he found his niche and his genius was recognized. And, as I discovered, he's not alone in that. Wiels showed me a much bigger world than I'd ever imagined I'd see, and I discovered it was populated by a whole lot of regular people living extraordinary lives. My association with him helped bring me even more famous clients, including Harrison Ford, Steve Ross, Priscilla Presley, George Lucas, and many others. I saw them all naked of any pretense too, and I came to understand that they had nothing on me. Or on you either!

> *You may or may not have a college degree but I'll bet you have a dream.*

They may be a little farther along on the success ladder and a little higher up the tax bracket, but from what I saw while sweating with the stars—and since—there is less separating you from fame and fortune than you probably think.

This book is going to get you pumped up to take care of business. You may or may not have a college degree but I'll bet you have a dream. I was the same way. I like to think that I had street smarts even if I didn't have a diploma on the wall. The truth is, I probably was more lucky than smart in those early days, but I got smarter as I went along. I listened to some wise people and I listened to my gut too.

In the pages that follow, I'm going to pass along to you what I've learned so that you too can become a street-smart success as an entrepreneur. Your star may not hang over Hollywood, but believe me, there are plenty of other businesses besides show business. Whatever it is that you want to do with your life, I'm here to tell you that if you believe it, you can achieve it.

Maybe you've been working for someone else and you're ready to reap the full benefits of your hard work and talent by creating your own business. Maybe you've been laid off, downsized, or otherwise put out of work. Don't waste another minute worrying or being angry. Instead of getting mad, get started on your very own business. Use that energy to build your life around doing something you love!

No matter where you are now, or where you've been, you can start over and build the life that you want for yourself. That's the naked truth. I've seen hundreds and even thousands of examples of regular people overcoming incredible challenges to build great lives for themselves and their families.

> *If you've been laid off or otherwise put out of work, don't*
> *get angry. Get started on your* own business.

Let me just give you the *Cliff Notes* version of my own background so you understand where I come from, which is probably a lot like where you come from and maybe even where you are right now.

Nobody stamped "future millionaire" on my birth certificate. I was so average that Gallup could have saved millions by polling just me. I was the sort of kid that parents charitably described as "stocky," and I had a terrible stutter. Still, I was an outgoing kid with a lot of pals, but back then I never would have dreamed that one day I'd be able to appear on television talking to millions of people. Just standing in front of the class and reading was a nightmare for me. I could read to myself just fine, but when I tried to say the words I couldn't get them out. It was embarrassing and frustrating and it turned me off school. My stutter was a curse and I don't say that lightly. For years, I didn't say anything lightly. Still, I didn't feel bad about myself. I'm just naturally an upbeat sort of guy.

I felt like I was never going to be the smart kid because I couldn't express myself, so instead, I filled the funny-fat-kid role. I wasn't obese, but I knew my way around the Twinkie rack. Even so, I was a fairly athletic and active kid. I played sports and I had friends who appreciated my sense of humor. I was thirteen years old and weighed 180 pounds—five-feet-five, squared—when my Mom took me to Syms clothing store on Long Island to get a suit for my bar mitzvah. I didn't get it when the salesman sized me up as a "Husky."

He led me and my Mom into an area where the suits were more like shower curtains with pockets and buttons. Then he handed me a blue suit that could have done double duty as a car cover. It had a "Husky" label sewn on a sleeve.

"What does that mean?" I asked my Mom.

"It means you are a young man now," she said kindly.

Cool! I thought. *I'm man-sized!*

On the morning of my bar mitzvah, my Mom had to promise me a month's worth of allowance money in advance to get me to take off the Husky label on the sleeve. I was happy with who I was because, at that point, I didn't know better.

Extreme Jakeover

Like most kids back then, all I knew about bodybuilding was what I read in the back pages of the comic books: those old Charles Atlas advertisements where the scrawny guy pumps up to kick tail after the bully kicks sand in his face at the beach. My dad tried to get me interested in weight lifting my freshman year in high school. He was a Navy veteran and a pretty tough guy with a soft heart. I'm sure he thought that if I built myself up a bit it would help me get my weight and my stutter under control. He set up a weight bench in the backyard and invited me out to learn how to do some basic training with free weights. I wasn't really interested. I still didn't get it at that point.

My father knew this was something I would have to decide to do for myself. He didn't get on my case. He just left the weight bench and free weights out in the yard in case I changed my mind. They sat out there most of the summer, killing the grass. Finally, in the fall, my Dad told me to move the weights and bench to the basement of our split-level house. I put them in a laundry room area just off my bedroom in the basement. Again, they just sat there like dead weight. I probably stepped over them or around them ten times every day.

Sometimes, in life and in business, all the tools we need to succeed are just sitting there waiting for us to discover them. It may be something that exists around us, or something that exists within us. Until we reach out and put those tools to work, we just exist in this world. But once we make that effort, we become part of the dynamic that drives the world!

Honestly, I think I finally went over and picked up the easy-curl bar because I was bored with social studies one night at the beginning of eighth grade at Baldwin Junior High School. I can still see myself putting the book down, getting out of bed and wandering around the basement in a tank top with my belly lapping over my pajama pants. I'd been listening to my headphones while I studied, and it may have been Frank Sinatra who got me motivated to get up. He was singing "My Way" when I picked up the two barbells and stood in front of a full length mirror.

> *Sometimes all the tools we need to succeed are just sitting there waiting for us to discover them.*

The kicker, though, was the very end of the song, after Ol' Blue Eyes stops singing. It was a "recorded live" album so there is this long and loud ovation, wild cheering and foot stomping that goes on and on. As I did my first set of biceps curls, I fantasized that those cheers and applause were for me. I started doing biceps curls with the barbells as 50,000 fans cheered "Jake! . . . Jake! . . . Jake!" in Madison Square Garden. That was a big moment, because my focus changed from thinking about how tough it was to do weight training to thinking about the rewards it might bring.

A Wish vs. a Decision

When I remember that moment, it occurs to me that it not only marked the beginning of my dedication to health and fitness, it also may have marked the start of my life as a business entrepreneur. I never would have accom-

plished all that I've done with my businesses if I'd dwelled on the problems
and challenges of starting them. But once I adjusted my attitude and became
more oriented toward solutions, a world of opportunities opened up.

The early teen years can be cruel, but I remember mine as fascinating,
because in my own small pre-adolescent way I was reinventing myself. I
began reading all of the weight-training magazines and books I could find,
and as my body responded, my entire physical and mental self-image got a
makeover worthy of a reality television show. That first session in my basement has remained so clear in my mind because it was a life-changing moment. It is probably no surprise either that I have a series of equally clear
memories of the days and weeks that followed. These are all "Kodak moments" imprinted in my memory as both my mind and body underwent
transformations.

> *Instead of dwelling on the problems of starting a
> business, orient yourself toward solutions, and a world of
> opportunities will open up.*

Scientists say that the brain literally rewires itself during our teen years.
New synapses, or connections, form to expand our ability to reason, calculate, and—for teenagers anyway—play video games. This rewiring process,
they say, explains why teens need so much sleep, why they tend to become
night owls, and why they sometimes seem to be in a total fog. It may also
explain why my memories of that time are so clear. My mind and body were
being rewired at the same time. When I began rewiring my body with weight
training, I felt differently about myself immediately.

This new sense of my own destiny revved me up as if I'd just drank a
triple tall dry cappuccino at Starbucks. I began to walk more confidently and
dress more neatly. I tucked my shirt in instead of letting it hang out to cover
my belly. I kept my chest out and shoulders back. I could feel my muscles
growing tighter and bigger. First the guys noticed, and then the girls started
commenting. It was like someone switched the background of my life from
black and white to living color. With high definition and surround sound.

Better yet, I became much more focused and in control. I worked out every night. I sent away for Charles Atlas' book, *Muscles in Seven Days*, but I never got it—and I'm still waiting! Weight training at that age produces results quickly and dramatically. My high school years were a lot more fun because of the confidence I gained. Once I'd started whipping my body in shape and trading flab for muscle, my stuttering all but disappeared too.

> *You can't just wish for success. A wish changes nothing;*
> *a decision changes everything.*

What does this have to do with helping you become a street-smart success? Some people claim that entrepreneurs are born, not made. I believe we live in a world full of success stories just waiting to be written. That's based not only on my own experiences but on those of countless other successful people I've known over the years. I've heard story after story of men and women who have overcome the most incredible challenges and who, as entrepreneurs, have found the most amazing ways to succeed in businesses that I didn't even know existed. I'll share many of their stories with you throughout this book. But, certainly it is true that if someone with my background—a regular guy with no college degree and no family money—can live a rich and rewarding life doing work that he loves, so can you.

I'm sure that you've probably heard many recipes for success already. I think success really boils down to something very basic, though certainly not simple. Above all else, you have to make the decision that success is yours to claim. You can't just wish for it. A wish changes nothing, a decision changes everything. There is no doubt in my mind that my own basic decision to keep picking up those barbells changed the course of my life.

Welcome to My Guide for Street-Smart Success!

Today, I am widely known by my *Body By Jake* brand of health and fitness products advertised on television, but you should think of this book as *Business By Jake*. I decided to write it after, somewhat to my surprise, I was invited to speak to business classes at several major colleges, including Stanford, Columbia, and New York University. In talking to the students at those big-time business schools, it dawned on me that even MBA professors realize that self-taught entrepreneurs have a unique perspective and special insights into the nitty-gritty of starting, running, growing, and surviving a business.

Still, even I was shocked when I spoke at Stanford University's Business School's Center for Entrepreneurial Studies. The lecture hall was packed! I mean, I know I'm a popular guy but after I heard that Warren Buffett was speaking just down the hall at the same time, I figured I'd be lucky to get a couple janitors in my audience. But we both packed 'em in!

I'm normally pretty charged up anyway, but the people in my audience energized me with their enthusiasm for the information I shared with them about my businesses. I explained how I built upon my one-man shop as the guy who created the personal fitness training business in Hollywood to create a global multi-media health and fitness empire. I told them that I'm still at it, growing my business and expanding my brand with new ventures in television and major league sports.

Admit it. You thought I was just a pretty face with a great body. Get over that. I've been fooling you. I'm really an entrepreneur with a pretty face and a great sense of humor! *Body By Jake* Global LLC is a nationally known health and fitness company focused on developing and marketing home exercise products through the direct response market. It was founded in 1990.

The business grew out of my early career as the first personal fitness trainer to the stars in Hollywood in the 1980s. I made a good living training celebrities and entertainment industry leaders, and I had a great time doing it. But thanks to my exposure to some of the keenest entrepreneurial minds in show business, I developed a greater vision for my life.

Like anybody else exposed to that seductive world, I had dreams of making it as an actor and I had some success doing that. But I also learned that the happiest people are those who build their lives around their natural interests and talents. I've enjoyed my occasional work in movies and had a great time during my four-year television series, *Big Brother Jake*, but ever since I started working out in my basement bedroom in our house on Long Island, I've enjoyed being involved in things that promote a healthier, positive lifestyle. I can't think of a more rewarding field of work—at least not one that I fit into so well.

I still get teased by fitness-minded stars like Faye Dunaway, who says my $200-per-half-hour rates drove up the price of good health in Hollywood, but I learned that my successful clients were willing to pay well for expert guidance that was motivational, fun, and produced results! My experiences in Hollywood proved to me that busy men and women around the country were a prime market for quality fitness equipment of all kinds. With that thought in mind, I began developing and marketing home fitness products carrying the *Body By Jake* brand. Today, we've invested more than $190 million in television and print advertising to promote our brand, generating more than $600 million in retail sales to over 4 million customers.

We've also been pioneers and leaders in the infomercial industry, where we've won a bunch of industry awards, and we've had a very lucrative partnership with the Home Shopping Network. We also operate our own television production division, *Body By Jake* Productions, which grew out of FIT TV, a 24-hour health and fitness cable channel I created in 1993. It was sold four years later for $500 million to Rupert Murdoch's Fox/Liberty Networks.

A Major League Move

Because our brand has become one of the world's most trusted and recognized names in the fitness industry, we are still exploring new ways to expand it with our own lines of clothing, shoes, and other items. My latest venture outside the *Body By Jake* global corporation is the most exciting and challenging entrepreneurial move I've ever made. This one will be a book all on its own one day. And I am betting my buttissimo that it will be one of the greatest success stories in sports history. I'll share the details of its birth and growth with you throughout this book too, but for now I'll just say that I am having a ball after opening up a whole new world of opportunities and adventures as founder of Major League Lacrosse, the nation's first professional outdoor lacrosse league.

I loved playing lacrosse, America's oldest game, in high school and during my brief college career, and now I'm dedicated to making it America's "freshest" national sport, with fast-paced, high-scoring, hard-hitting action. I launched Major League Lacrosse in June of 2000 as a single-entity ownership structure to showcase the best professional outdoor lacrosse in the world, with my partners Dave Morrow, a legendary Princeton lacrosse player who founded Warrior Lacrosse equipment company, and Tim Robertson, my friend and former partner in FitTV.

The league, which plays May through August, began with six teams located in Baltimore, Boston, Long Island, New Jersey, Philadelphia, and Rochester, New York, and by 2006 we plan to expand to six more cities in the western United States. To operate a team, owners had to put up $600,000, and as of this writing, the value is $1.5 million to purchase the operating rights. I'm really pumped up that in just our first four years we've been able to line up a television deal with ESPN, and we've secured official partnership deals with major players that include Gatorade, Tommy Hilfiger, 24 Hour Fitness, Sporting News, Joe Boxer, Cascade Sports Helmets, Sony Pictures, Starbucks, Paramount, and Great Atlantic Lacrosse Company. We've also got multiyear sponsorship deals with Anheuser-Busch (Bud Light), New Balance, Warrior, and Under Armour.

I've done some heavy lifting in my time, but creating from scratch an entire professional sports league is by far the greatest and most exciting challenge I've ever undertaken. If being an entrepreneur means learning how to manage risk, then I've entered the major leagues in that department too. I will share stories of what I've learned, and what I am still learning from this unique start-up, which has given the Jake-ster more chills and thrills than anything I've ever done.

No Limit Living

In my bodybuilding days, I was always pushing to set a new "max" by pressing, benching, and lifting more and more weight. The fact is that your body can only lift so much before the muscles max out. That's why I enjoy being a businessman so much. There is no max. No ceiling. You are limited only by your imagination and your energy.

> *Cash flow is life blood to most businesses. But money doesn't lead. It follows.*

What about money? No doubt about it, money is critically important. Cash flow is life blood to most businesses. But money doesn't lead. It follows. What does it follow? Wealth follows creativity. It follows street smarts. It

follows team work. It follows energy. It follows resilience. It follows fearless-
ness. And it follows a Don't Quit attitude.

Those are lessons I want to share with you in this book. My business
success offers you a real life, real world example because, when you get right
down to it, I built a multi-million dollar empire with starting assets that
boiled down to a towel, a broomstick, and a chair!

Before we get rolling, I'd like to ask you to make that decision right now.
Stop wishing for what you want. Start deciding what you are going to do to
get it. While you think about that, here are a few enticements to consider.

Five Reasons for Seeking Street-Smart Success

1. MAKE YOUR OWN RULES!

There are a lot of standard business practices that I won't be offering advice
about in this book. Things like the 9-to-5 workday, proper business attire,
office politics, and working your way up the chain of command aren't part
of the street-smart business plan. And that's a good thing.

Freedom to make your own rules, or no rules at all, is the greatest thing
about being your own boss. I've punched a clock a few times in my life, and
I always felt like a bird checking into its cage. (Me as a canary, now there's a
visual you might not want to think about too long.) But most days when I'm
in Los Angeles, I come into the office around noon or later after an early
workout in my home gym, a few quiet hours in my home office making
business phone calls and reading, and breakfast with my wife and kiddies. I
get a lot done before I ever leave the house.

When I head in to my office in Los Angeles, I usually wear jeans, a Polo
shirt, and tennis shoes. Most of our employees dress in whatever style makes
them feel comfortable in the office—which may include ski parkas and
gloves since I like to keep the AC at "Arctic." Still, just because we don't
follow a lot of corporate formalities doesn't mean that we run a loose ship.
We rock and roll. But we do have fun. I love what I do and I want my
employees to love their jobs too. We don't need rules to keep us focused,
we're already honed in. I work long hours. I do appearances on the Home
Shopping Network on many weekends, and sometimes I'm on a plane every

day of the week. But I'm my own boss. I reap the full rewards of my work. And I feel good about everything we are involved in because it promotes a healthy lifestyle for our customers.

It's a great way to live, which is why I'm encouraging you to put your street smarts to work too!

2. STAY PUMPED UP!

In one recent twenty-minute stretch at the office, I:

- Looked through photographs of mansions in Hawaii that we were considering for an infomercial shoot.

- Brainstormed with the commissioner of Major League Lacrosse about expansion cities.

- Talked on the telephone with Deion Sanders and his gorgeous wife Pilar about coming to their house near Dallas to tape their endorsement for one of our new fitness products.

The only thing I don't accomplish in a typical day is boredom. Every entrepreneur I know feels the same way. We don't get bored because if things start to get boring in one business, we go start another! Most of us have so many irons in the fire that we have to hire professional managers to take care of the nitty-gritty details. That way we stay pumped up about building our businesses and finding fresh opportunities.

My father was a good man who became trapped in a bad job late in life. I watched him lose interest in his work, and then, sadly, he lost his vitality and his sense of accomplishment. It affected his relationships and his health. I'm sure you've seen it happen to people you know and care about. I became determined that I would never get into the same situation. I don't want it to happen to you either. Life's too short.

If you don't look forward to going to work most days, then you should find other work. Most people are happiest when they are working for themselves, doing what they love to do, applying all of their energy and creativity and brain power to something that fulfills them. Some people can get pumped up working for someone else, and that's great for them. But for people like me—and you too, I'll bet—there is nothing as stimulating as being in the driver's seat. Day in and day out, you want to stay excited about what you do and the contributions you make to the world around you. Success isn't about money flowing into the bank. It's about what flows through your heart and keeps it pumping!

> *If you don't look forward to going to work most days, then you should find other work.*

3. MAKE A MARK!

Have you priced a pyramid lately? Labor costs and limestone blocks have gone through the roof! So, it's really not practical to build a monument to yourself like King Tut. All those pesky tourists climbing around can really drive up your insurance rates too. So to fulfill that basic human need to make a mark on the world, building a business is a better way to go.

Psychologists say that as social beings we are all driven to be part of something bigger than ourselves. That's why most of us are naturally drawn to neighborhood groups, clubs, and communities. It is also part of our nature to want to create something that contributes to society and impacts it in a beneficial way. When you use your street smarts to create a business, you add to the richness of your community. Economists often say that entrepreneurs and business owners are the lifeblood of this country because we add jobs, pay taxes, provide products and services that generate more jobs, taxes, products, and services.

> *Starting your own business isn't just about making a living, it's about making a mark!*

We run lean at *Body By Jake* Global LLC. We've only got fifteen people in the office. It's a family and, I've got to tell you, when one of the people in the office talks about buying a house or getting a new car, we all feel good because we know that this business we've created and grown is helping to make their lives better too. That's just a great feeling! Starting your own business isn't just about making a living, it's about making a mark!

4. GET IN THE GAME!

When you have your own business, you become a player in your community. You are no longer in the stands or on the bench, you are in the most economically important game. Your business, whether big or small, is also part of the much larger economic and social engine that keeps things running. It's not like you go to the office every day thinking, "I'm going to contribute a chunk of cash to the gross national product in a big way today!" But it's no joke that people who start their own businesses are a vital part of the world's economy.

One scholarly study found that entrepreneurship is a major contributing factor to a country's economic well being, both in terms of economic growth and job creation. It accounted for roughly one-third of the difference in growth rates among the ten countries analyzed by researchers from Babson College, the London Business School, and the Kauffman Center for Entrepreneurial Leadership. Michael Hay, a professor at the London Business School who participated in the study, noted in it that "entrepreneurship makes a difference to economic prosperity and that a country without high business start-up rates is risking economic stagnation."

So street-smart and book-smart folks agree: Being in business means getting off the sidelines and getting in the game!

5. DON'T QUIT!

I've never met a retired entrepreneur, and that gives me hope for the future. The thought of retiring and checking into Happy Trails Village and joining the shuffleboard team has no appeal to me now, and I don't think it will appeal to me when I'm seventy years old either. I want to go down kicking. I want to stay in the game because I'm always going to keep it fun. Now that doesn't mean I look forward to doing *Body By Jake* Prune Juice infomercials while wobbling in a walker . . . hey, that's not a bad idea! When the time is right, I'll pass my existing businesses on to my children, or at least to the next generation of street-smart folks. But I do intend to keep generating ideas and chasing them for as long as I can because being an entrepreneur means you don't ever have to quit. There is no mandatory retirement age for enjoying your work.

| *I've never met a retired entrepreneur.*

A 1998 survey of baby boomers by the American Association of Retired Persons found that 80 percent of respondents planned to work beyond retirement age, and 17 percent of them planned to launch new businesses. Another recent study found that 22 percent of men and 14 percent of women over 65 are self-employed. That's compared to a lowly 7 percent for other age groups. Researchers at Vanderbilt University predict that the number of entrepreneurs age 45 to 64 will increase by 15 million by 2006 while they expect a decline of 4 million for entrepreneurs age 25 to 44.

Yet another report, "Third Age Entrepreneurs" by Barclays Bank, found that older entrepreneurs are responsible for 50 percent more business start-ups than ten years ago—with about 60,000 business start-ups in 2003 alone.

Of course, nobody's saying that you have to keep working, but take this as a warning: Once you get cooking, doing your own thing, using all your creativity and know-how, spending every day as your own boss, having fun, creating jobs, and contributing to the community, you won't want to quit either. The world lets you be what you make them believe you are! So make your own rules and keep rocking until the old rocking chair falls off the porch! It's that simple. It's that great!

So, what do you say? Let's get down to business!

2

street smarts

MY FAMILY MOVED from Long Island to suburban Los Angeles shortly after I went West to pursue my bodybuilding career. My parents were worried about my choice of career. They thought my goal of becoming Mr. America was pretty shaky, mostly because they didn't see how I'd be able to feed myself or pay the bills. So, my father tried to get me interested in his business. He had a local magazine, sort of a shopper and real estate guide. He wanted to groom me as his advertising sales guy. I didn't find that very appealing, but I appreciated what he was trying to do for me. So when he asked me to give it a try, I went along with it.

He'd made an appointment for me to call on one of his regular clients, a florist who had advertised in his magazine. I didn't know it then, but I was being set up. My father had promised the florist a free ad if he'd make me work hard to make the sale. The idea was to get my competitive juices going so that I'd see how much fun it could be to be a magazine advertising salesman instead of training to be Mr. America! You gotta love a father who cares enough to do something like that. But there was one major problem. I had no interest in that line of work, and so it really didn't matter to me whether Mr. FTD bought an ad or not.

I admired my father for starting his magazine. I thought he was a great salesman and a hard-working guy. But I've never been a suit-and-tie kind of guy. If I button my shirt all the way up the veins in my neck stand out and my face turns lava red!

Building abs, not selling ads, was my thing. My interests then were entirely focused on building biceps the size of coconuts. Still, I did it for Dad. I suited up, tucked his magazine and sales materials under my arm and went to the flower shop.

Following the script my father had provided, I pitched the owner on an $800 ad inside the front cover.

"No, thanks," the florist said, following the script my father had given him.

"Okay, thanks," I said. Then I headed out the door.

My father was shocked when I returned to his office.

"You gave up that easily?" he asked.

"The guy said no thanks, was I supposed to beat him with a bridal bouquet to make him change his mind?"

"Of course he said no, you putz, I told him to make you work for it a little so your competitive juices would get flowing!" my father said.

| *You've got to do what interests you.*

That was the end of my association with his business. He gave up on ever bringing me into the fold as an ad salesman. He recognized that I had a talent for sales and marketing, but like a wise parent, he knew I'd have to find my own way of expressing that talent.

"You've got to do what interests you," he said. And he was right!

Take a Meeting

Before we get started on building your street-smart success, I want you to have a serious sit down with the person who will play the most important role in its creation.

Take a look in the mirror and say hello.

Before you can sell anybody else on your dream, you've got to sell your-self. You've got to be certain that this is what you want to do. You've got to know in your heart, in your gut and in the tips of your toenails that you want to build your life around this business.

Why is that important? Because I don't want you looking in the mirror when you are sixty-five years old and thinking: I should have done some-thing I enjoyed more. I want you to love what you do day in and day out so that you never look back and wish you'd taken another path.

So take a meeting with yourself and ask: Is this it? Does just thinking about doing it pump you up? When you visualize your business do you immediately see all sorts of opportunities for growing it and expanding it?

> *When you are sixty-five years old, you don't want to be thinking, I should have done something I enjoyed more.*

If you can't see beyond a few days or weeks or months, you aren't dream-ing big enough. And don't get too wrapped up in dollar signs at this point. Sure, you want your business to be profitable. I hope you make millions. But don't do it for the dough. Do it because it feels good. If you love what you do, I believe your fortune will follow. Maybe your rewards will come with dead presidents pictured on them, or maybe there will be other re-wards, like the satisfaction of creating something that makes the world a better place, or that eases the lives of other people.

Whatever the rewards, you can't go wrong if you put your street smarts and your talents and drive towards something that excites you and makes you jump out of bed every morning.

It's got to be that way because there will be days when it won't be easy. You've got to love it enough that when all you hear is "no," you'll keep going until you find a "yes."

Believe me, your pal Jake knows "no." I heard it in every possible way and in several different languages when I began pitching the idea of Major League Lacrosse.

No, it's not a big enough sport.

No, it doesn't translate on TV.

No, people don't understand the rules.

I heard "no" until it was coming out my nose.

And do you *know* what? I'm still hearing it even though we're in our fifth season and still growing! If I'd listened to all the people who told me "no" I'd still be back in Baldwin trying to muscle my way through life.

So hear me when I'm telling you that you've got to love it so much that when the phone doesn't ring, you pick it up and make things happen. (This doesn't include calling yourself, by the way.)

I've packed this book with information that will help you become a street-smart success with the business of your dreams. But I can't reach into your heart and adjust the horizontal and vertical. So before we get started, you've got to make sure you've got a clear picture of what you want.

Ask yourself these questions and write down your answers just to be certain:

- Is this something I want to do every day of the week?

- Can I see myself doing this for the next five, ten, or twenty years?

- Will I be able to sell this idea to investors, partners, or employees?

- Do I see endless opportunities coming out of this idea?

- Will this be so much fun I won't want to take days off?

- Is it the sort of thing I'll be proud to be a part of?

- Does it match up with my interests?

- Would I do this even if nobody paid me?

- Is it such an exciting thing that nobody can talk me out of it?

If you answered "no" to any of those questions, I want you to do something street smart. Not for me, but for yourself and your future sanity. Before you go ahead with this idea, go to work for somebody who has a similar business. Check it out. Spend at least six months seeing how it feels, tastes, smells, and sounds. If at the end of that period, your no has turned into a yes, then get rolling!

You and the Universe

Once you get tuned in to a business that suits your soul, I'm telling you, something very strange and wonderful occurs. When street-smart types chase their dreams and build their lives around things they love to do, good stuff happens. Opportunities appear. It's like the whole universe opens up to you in really wild ways. I'm not trying to sound like Deepak Steinfeld here. I don't know Chopra from Oprah. But just look at what happened to me.

There I was, doing my thing as a fitness trainer with a few people around Hollywood when I got this unbelievable phone call to work with Steven Spielberg. Back then in 1981, I was still thinking like a bodybuilder, not like a businessman. I had what Deepak and Dr. Phil might call a "limited vision" for my life. That's something you have to watch out for. You'll never make it as an entrepreneur if you consciously or unconsciously place limits on what you can do. There was a famous architect and city planner, Daniel Burnham, whose motto was, "Make no little plans." I like that. Here's how he put it: "Make no little plans. They have no magic to stir men's blood . . . Make big plans; aim high in hope and work."

Just saying that opens things up for you, doesn't it? No. It doesn't. Just saying it may get you thinking along the right track, but you have to live it. That's what I learned while working with many of the entertainment indus-try's true entrepreneurial wizards. They may joke about it as "La-La Land," but believe me—those huge mansions in Beverly Hills aren't the homes of idle dreamers or people who think small. And most of the people who live in them weren't born there. They got there by relentlessly chasing their dreams and by daring to think there were no limits on what they could do.

> *Little plans have no magic to stir men's blood. Make big plans.*

And you know what else? They don't quit! Even when they've got enough money to buy their own islands, they keep looking for new opportunities to pursue their interests and passions. Many of the most creative people I know in Hollywood never stop looking for opportunities to do what they love to do. That's how I ended up in a starring role in an unreleased Steven Spielberg movie that even his most fervent fans have never heard about, let alone seen. And if certain big stars and Hollywood executives have their way, it will never been seen!

This movie could be considered a sequel to *Jaws* minus the shark, but with plenty of stomach-churning moments. Wiels made it on a fishing trip that we took with Richard Dreyfuss and a few other Hollywood hotshots, who will ban me from Beverly Hills if I reveal their names. We were on a charter boat when a storm hit and turned the ocean into a giant whirly. I was lucky. I might have suffered the same fate, except for the fact that Wiels took this opportunity to stick the video camera in my face while he played the evil director: "Okay, Jake, let the Puke Monster jump on you!"

It was a good thing I resisted Spielberg's seafaring direction. A few weeks after the perfect storm fishing trip, he had a party in which he screened his limited-run film. It'll never be a critical favorite or a box office hit, but if nothing else, this movie proves that Wiels will take any opportunity to pick up a camera and do his thing!

Street-smart entrepreneurs are every bit as obsessed with their passion for doing business. I speak from experience. My name is Jake and I'm a serial entrepreneur. My earnings from the sale of the FitTV cable channel to Rupert Murdoch's Fox/Liberty Networks were enough to take care of me and my family for the rest of our lives. I could have handed the dough off to an investment firm, moved the wife and kids to Hawaii, found a nice place on the beach, and lived a life of luaus. Instead, I made a move that led some to conclude that I was certifiably crazy.

Looking back, I think it proved beyond a doubt that I am a certified street-smart success seeker. (By the way, many people would argue that the two are not mutually exclusive.) Rather than cashing out and saying aloha, I did what most entrepreneurs do naturally: I went shopping for a bigger and better opportunity. My friends and coworkers say that I am like a kid tossing handfuls of spaghetti at a wall to see what sticks. It's true. I constantly throw out ideas about potential business opportunities. Some of them stick to the wall and turn into a carbonara of cash!

Feast or famine, I'm an opportunity junkie. And that may be *the* most critical trait for street-smart success. I'm never content to have just one venture going on, even if it's going like gangbusters. I believe that one opportunity leads to another. Even if the door slams on one business idea, it often opens another door to a totally different opportunity. That's what happened in this case.

Shortly after I sold FitTV, there was a lot of buzz about minor league sports making a big comeback. Cash-rich folks in Hollywood were investing in minor league baseball teams in a big way. There were reports in the media and business and investment journals that disgruntled sports fans who could no longer afford the price of major league tickets were flocking to the smaller stadiums to watch minor league teams in places like Oklahoma City and Des Moines. I looked at a couple of business plans for minor league baseball teams, but nothing really excited me even though I had played Little League. The highlight of my baseball career was a four-hitter I pitched against a team sponsored by the Jewish War Veterans. I went out on top, retiring my mitt after that.

> *Even if the door slams on your business idea, it may open another door to a totally different opportunity.*

I did like the idea of getting involved in some sort of sporting venture but I put it on the back burner. I focused instead on another opportunity on my pasta plate. I'd been reading health and fitness magazines since junior high. After Martha Stewart had so much success with her magazine, it occurred to me that having my own *Body By Jake* magazine would be a great way to expand the brand. I sold the idea to David Pecker, who was then CEO of Hachette Filipacchi magazines, which published everything from *Car & Driver* to *Elle* to *George*. Then all we had to do was sell it to some big advertisers.

Remember what I said about one opportunity always leading to another? Well, this is a great example, and it's typical of the totally wacky way things work when street-smart folks keep their opportunity antennas in the air. I believe in pursuing opportunities with deep roots and long branches. I stay rooted in my core business, which is health and fitness, but I am always looking to branch out from that base. You won't see the *Body By Jake* brand on a vodka bottle, but you could see it on a sports drink someday. So, a health and fitness magazine fit into my concept of a great opportunity.

Magazine publishing is a tough business, though. Hundreds of new titles show up on the news racks every year, and very few survive beyond six months. People may need *People*, but the majority of magazines start-ups are extremely high risk. Selling subscriptions is important, but first you have to get the big-brand advertisers on board. They can make or break you.

Like a lot of entrepreneurial types, I'm a natural ham who loves making sales pitches, so I was only too happy to accompany David Pecker on a round of sales visits. It was a group outing for three of Hachette Filipacchi's magazines. And what a group it was. I found myself aboard the publisher's corporate jet with John Kennedy, Jr., who had launched *George* magazine, and Ralph Lauren's son David, who was pitching a new lifestyle magazine of his own, called *Swing*. We flew to Detroit that day to talk up our magazines to the advertising and marketing chiefs at General Motors and Ford.

Major League Opportunity

I had to field a lot of questions from the two younger guys during the trip because they were eager to get fashion and grooming tips from me. But when they weren't pestering me for the name of my hair stylist, I looked through samples of their magazines they'd brought along. One article in David's *Swing* caught my eye because it was about lacrosse, which I'd played in high school. I hadn't heard much about lacrosse since I left school, but this story caught my attention. It was a profile of David Morrow, a young former lacrosse star at Princeton, who had started a company called "Warrior Lacrosse." The story said that Morrow grew up in Detroit and that he was a hockey player before a teacher turned him onto lacrosse. At Princeton he'd struggled at first against more experienced competition, but he didn't quit (I knew I'd like this guy!). In fact, he became an All-American and won a national title.

Like most lacrosse stars, Dave played aggressively. His lacrosse sticks were always getting broken. He went to his father, a Detroit engineer, who helped him create a titanium lacrosse stick. It was lighter and stronger, and soon his teammates were asking for their own titanium sticks. David jumped on the opportunity and took it to the net. He started Warrior Lacrosse in 1993, and it quickly became the nation's leading producer of lacrosse equipment.

Reading the story about him, it seemed to me that this young guy was onto something with a lot of potential. I'd always felt that lacrosse had everything American sports fans love—lots of action, scoring, and physical contact. It had long been a popular sport in the eastern United States, but this article said it was growing in popularity across the Midwest and in the western and southern states too. High school and college kids were playing it in increasing numbers. There'd been several attempts to create a professional lacrosse league over the years. An indoor version had attracted fans to the sport and created a base, though most agreed that the indoor game didn't allow for the same athleticism and excitement as the more natural, outdoor version.

What really got my attention was that Dave Morrow wasn't just selling lacrosse sticks—he was marketing lacrosse as a lifestyle for the hip ESPN and extreme sports crowd. Before our plane touched the ground, I'd decided that this was an opportunity I wanted to explore.

Sixth Sense

All of the street-smart successes I've known had a sixth sense for spotting opportunities. It's almost like having ESP, or extra-sensory perception, but the focus is on business opportunities. (I guess if you find an opportunity in sports business you have ESPN?) Some people are born with great vision, but others develop it by training themselves to always stay alert for business opportunities and developing their own systems for finding them. Opportunities for street-smart success are everywhere, even in seemingly mundane everyday things like athletic shoes and lacrosse sticks.

Take a walk through your neighborhood shopping mall, check out the grocery store shelves, or look at the Chamber of Commerce membership list or the Yellow Pages in your phone book, and you'll see that opportunities come in all shapes and sizes. Opportunities really are everywhere you look. What, you don't believe me? Get out the door, you say? Meet my friend

Casey Laughlin, CEO of Exit, Inc. in Littleton, Colorado. His company makes exit signs, and believe me, it's a going concern. Somebody has to make them, right? From A to Z (aspirin to zippers?) products and services of all kinds offer business opportunities for street-smart success.

> *Opportunities for street-smart success are everywhere, even in seemingly mundane everyday things.*

Some products may hit the shelves as unique ideas—like personal computers or iPods—creating entirely new industries. Others are based in new technologies or more creative marketing for existing concepts, like Warrior's lighter, stronger lacrosse sticks, or Mrs. Field's cookies.

Uncommon Opportunities

A guy named James Murdock stuck his head underwater and found an opportunity. He took something that has been around forever, simple swimming pools, and created a $25 million dollar business by coming up with a whole new spin on them. He is the founder of Endless Pools, which makes home lap pools that create currents for people who swim for exercise.

Murdock saw an opportunity where other people just saw water. What could be more common than swimming pools? How about a cup of coffee? I love high-octane java *and* I'm a big fan of great entrepreneurial concepts, which is why nearly every morning I stop by Starbucks for a double tall dry cappuccino with a splash of milk and a lot of foam. Then, most afternoons I go back for my own special grande caramel frappedoo!

Starbucks is a great entrepreneurial business launched by a street-smart guy who saw opportunity in a cup of joe! I love it so much I went to Seattle to meet with founder Howard Schultz and his chief marketing officer, Ann Saunders. We hit it off and now Starbucks is a sponsor for Major League Lacrosse (MLL)!

As your career as a street-smart entrepreneur develops and grows, you'll find yourself drawn to men and women who are opportunity junkies just like you. And sometimes you'll end up creating even more opportunities together, as Howard Schultz and I have done with our sponsorship deal between MLL and Starbucks. Just as I created the professional outdoor lacrosse league after seeing an opportunity for a sport that I'd always enjoyed, Howard poured his love of coffee into a global business. He was the New York-based U.S. sales chief for Hammarplast Swedish drip coffeemakers in the early 1980s, when he went to Seattle to check out a local coffee-bean store called Starbucks, which had become a big seller of his coffeemakers. The owners were coffee connoisseurs who impressed him with their knowledge and dedication to their customers. He also fell in love with Seattle's laid back atmosphere, so he decided to go to work for Starbucks, as their director of marketing and operations.

When he joined the company, Starbucks sold only coffee beans and equipment. They didn't brew it in their retail stores. But after a business trip to Italy in 1982, Howard came home with an idea that transformed the Seattle company into a global brand. In Italy, there were coffee bars on nearly every block—200,000 of them across the country—where customers sat drinking great espresso, talking, reading and having informal meetings. The coffee shops were part of Italian society! Howard loved that, but his bosses at Starbucks said they didn't want to get into the restaurant business. Did Howard Schultz give up on his great idea? No! Instead, Howard started his own coffee bar called Il Giornale. It went over like gangbusters and a year later, he bought Starbucks from its original owners for $3.8 million!

From then on, his goal was to build a company whose coffee bars not only sold great coffee, but also had the soul of those Italian neighborhood meeting places. He now has more than 3,300 stores around the world and employs more than 40,000 people. When I visited Howard at Starbucks headquarters in Seattle just recently, he introduced me to his board of managers. I flashed my Starbucks card at them and they all cheered! We're going to do great things together.

The success of Howard Schultz at Starbucks—which is really a similar story to that of Ray Kroc, the former milk shake machine salesman who turned the McDonald's family restaurant into a global brand—illustrates that there are opportunities for incredible entrepreneurial success even in existing businesses. Many street-smart successes have found their first opportunities by buying an established shop or business. Others have gotten into the game by purchasing a franchise like Subway or Mailboxes Etc. You have to decide which type of opportunity suits you best. Each has its upsides and downsides. Some involve higher levels of risk than others.

Buying an existing business means that you'll probably have an established market for your product or service, but it might also mean that opportunities for expansion and growth could be more limited. There are thousands of people who've built substantial wealth by getting in early on hot franchise opportunities, but there are also many who've felt stifled and frustrated by the tight controls and financial demands made by the corporations that control most franchises. You'll have to consider the advantages and disadvantages of each type of opportunity and figure out what will work for you.

There is a price of admission for every type of venture. Buying into an established franchise or business generally will cost you a considerable amount up front. The good thing about starting your own business is that you can usually control your up-front costs and grow the business at a comfortable pace—and you can be your own boss, make your own decisions, and reap the full benefits of your work. Of course, you also will have the full responsibility for financing, running, and guiding your business.

Build Your Business Around Your Interests

We all have to make a living and pay the bills. I encourage you to find a way to meet those responsibilities by doing something that truly excites and interests you. It's not just about making money. You will quickly find that your life is built around your business or career, so from the very start you'll want to make sure it is something that you can live with day in and day out. It's like being married. You wouldn't want to hook up with someone who only mildly interests you—at least I hope you wouldn't.

> *The long-term success of your business will depend largely on what you do with the opportunities that arise once it is up and running.*

The most successful street-smart successes look for opportunities that match up with their own interests when starting a business. But the opportunities don't end there. The long-term success of your business will largely depend on what you do with the opportunities that arise once it is up and running. Here are some likely ways to spot new opportunities once you've established a business.

1. SEARCHING FOR SOLUTIONS TO PROBLEMS

When challenges occur, street-smart successes don't react to the problems, they look for the opportunities that are created. At *Body By Jake,* we test our fitness products relentlessly before we offer them to our customers and clients. During the testing and evaluation process, we spot ways to make the products even better, and in some cases, ways that inspire entirely new products.

Every day, we receive samples and proposals from fitness equipment inventors and manufacturers who want us to sell their products under our brand name. We see some fantastic stuff, and some really wild concepts too. But we do check out everything because you never know when a real great opportunity will pop out of the UPS box. One of the wackier ideas we've seen for a piece of fitness equipment was a product I'll call "Fatty Clamps." It was a device that the customer was supposed to clamp onto love handles and other excess customer parts.

We didn't think people would be too excited about spending $19.95 to be reminded that they were . . . well . . . fat. But I was so blown away by the sheer insanity of that idea that I had to meet the Fatty Clamp guy and hear his pitch. When he came in, he had the passion and drive that it takes to turn an idea into a business, but Fatty Clamps wasn't the right opportunity—at least not for us. Now if he'd been selling a new sports car, or a real quality piece of fitness equipment, I might have bought it because I loved the enthusiasm of the Fatty Clamps guy, even though his product didn't do it for me or anyone else at *Body By Jake.*

But it's also true that one of our most recent hits came as the result of looking at other products that sparked something in my mind. I'd been looking at several rough prototypes for new fitness equipment. They each had their good points, but none of them was strong enough to capture my interest. Still, in looking at them, an idea occurred to me. The problem with most of the machines I'd been looking at was that they were too limited, too bulky, or just didn't deliver enough for the price.

In studying those problems in other products, I came up with an idea for an entirely new machine. We'd seen a lot of machines designed for abdominal crunches to work the upper abdominal muscles. We'd seen other machines designed to work the lower abs, and still a third type of machine that worked the oblique muscles along the sides of the trunk. We'd had two products designed for abs that had done very well in the past, but it occurred to me that we'd never seen or sold a machine that worked both upper and lower abdominals and oblique muscles to really develop that "six pack" look.

It also had hit me that all of our products used resistance bands, weight stacks, or bungee chords to create the necessary stress to build muscle. Those items added cost and bulk to our machines. But what if we used the person's own bodyweight to create that same stress?

We contacted an inventor-engineer in Minneapolis who'd worked on other products for us and ran my ideas past him. We gave him some specific ideas about what was required of this product, and we told him to see what he could come up with. In a few months, we had the basic concepts for the Ab Scissor, which has been the most successful product in the history of our company. We have done more than $100 million in sales with that product, and the market is still growing. Customers write or call us nearly every day telling us what a difference it has made for them.

2. CUSTOMER OR CLIENT FEEDBACK

I am a huge believer in always taking every phone call, answering every e-mail. That may sound too good to be true but in some way shape or form we do that. Really, it's not only about finding opportunities, it's also about giving other people a chance. Early in my career, I hoped that whenever I sent a note or a tape to someone I would get a response; when I didn't, I'd always say that one day—not *if* but *when* I had people pitching me with ideas—I would answer and respond. At *Body By Jake*, we have a great relationship with our customers. Often people buy every one of our products because they believe in them and they know we stand behind them.

It's gotten to the point that we are now using our customers in our infomercials. We recently filmed a new Ab Scissor infomercial in Hawaii—the first time we've done a second show for a product of our own—and there are ten customers in it. We put out a call on our Web site and we got 60,000 responses. We chose ten special customers and flew them and their spouses to Hawaii for the taping because they'd each written us about their success with the product. We wanted to make them the stars of the show. These are people who bought our products while watching our show on television, and who used them for tremendous results! It was great to meet them and to hear their suggestions. Their enthusiasm and support inspires us to keep working to find and develop the best products we can.

3. TECHNOLOGICAL DEVELOPMENTS

Lighter, stronger, faster, bouncier. . . . Bouncier? New technology probably creates more opportunities for street-smart folks than anything else. Look around you and you'll see how recent developments like wireless Internet networks and GPS—the global satellite system used in everything from car navigation and security systems to hiking, yacht racing, and farming—have created all sorts of opportunities for new products and businesses that have changed the way we live.

The fitness field has benefited from lighter and stronger materials over the years. To stay on top of technological developments you should read the newsletters and check out the Web sites related to your field, from professional organizations to trade shows and special interest forums on the Internet. Even if you led your chemistry class in broken beakers, you'll learn to appreciate technological developments that impact your business. And who says scientists can't be fun to hang out with?

Bouncier? Meet Norman Stigley, a chemical engineer who got his kicks by playing around with synthetic rubber molecules. When he combined polybutadiene and sulfur (two of *my* favorite afternoon snacks), he created a new compound called, are you ready for this? ZECTRON!!!

Hey, wake up! Any true street-smart sort will realize that there is opportunity in that thar' Zectron. Can you say SuperBalls? That's right. Bouncier! Ol' Norman sold his formula to the folks at Wham-o in the 1960s, and the SuperBall was born. More than 20 million were sold! And Norman Stigley bounced all the way to the bank!

4. SUPPLIER OR PARTNER INFORMATION

Because of our long-term relationships, honest dealings, and the many successes we've had, our relationship with our product manufacturing plants, distribution teams, and telemarketers is so good that we now operate as a finely tuned unit. We are true partners in success even though we are separate companies owned by different entities.

Believe me, it's not always like that. Many business owners will tell you that the companies that they depend upon to supply them with essential components or to manufacture, distribute, or market their products are a nightmare to deal with. It can be cutthroat out there, especially in a tough economy. Manufacturing companies often strong-arm their suppliers and distributors. Smaller companies get beat up by bigger businesses whose products or services they depend upon. We don't work that way. We're not pushovers, by any means. But we believe in fostering long-term relationships with our business partners and suppliers.

We've been selling products on the Home Shopping Network (HSN) for more than ten years now. We've grown together over the years. We've become far more sophisticated in our shows and HSN has advanced light years in their production capabilities. We have a great partnership that's benefited both businesses enormously. I go to their studios near Tampa, Florida, about ten times each year, and when I go on the air there, it's like ringing 80 million doorbells. It's just a fun way to do business because it is such a well-run, high-tech, and professional operation. We've sold millions of dollars in products on Home Shopping Network. We've profited. They've profited. And our customers and their viewers have profited.

We try to work it out so that everyone we do business with feels that they are treated fairly and with respect. We don't take advantage of anyone. And the benefits of that attitude include long-term financial success, because our partners and suppliers are invested in our success and we are invested in theirs. Those relationships create more opportunities for all of us.

I'd by lying to you if I said all of those opportunities pan out, but even those that turn out to be major flops can make for good stories. Several years ago we were offered a licensing deal by a New York manufacturer of skin- and hair-care products. This was back when I still had a fitness studio in Manhattan, and this company wanted us to sell *Body By Jake* shampoo in what we hoped would be a whole chain of fitness studios around the country.

Before we agreed to talk about the deal, we asked the shampoo maker to send us some samples. I then passed them around to the president of my company Phil Scotti, to my lawyer Bob Lieberman, and to a few other friends and family members. I tried my sample of *Body By Jake* shampoo the next morning in the shower. About twenty minutes later, my head started itching really bad. By the time I got to the office, there were phone messages from my itchy buddies, Bob and Phil. They'd tried the shampoo too, and both recommended that I "scratch" this deal!

5. A MARKET-SHIFTING EVENT

When Americans began to pay more attention to their eating habits, McDonalds, Wendy's and Burger King suffered because they weren't paying attention to that market shift. But the Subway fast-food chain found an opportunity to ride that market shift. It scored huge sales increases by introducing Jared Fogel, the young guy who dropped from a size-60 waistline to a size-34 waistline by eating only Subway sandwiches, hold the mayo. For more than three years, Subway's sales climbed. More recently, the chain introduced sandwiches from the Atkins diet to try and catch that market shift too.

> *There are always new opportunities in times of change, so do everything possible to be informed, primed, and ready to act.*

When the tide turns, you can either get swept under and drowned or you can catch a wave. That's why I read the entertainment, sports and fitness, and health trade papers and the daily newspapers too, to keep an eye out for shifting markets and fresh trends. Believe me, I also listen to my wife and her friends, to teenagers and to the television shows and channels they watch, like *MTV* and *The Game Show Network*. To stay ahead you have to know what young people are doing, right?

There are always opportunities to develop new products and new entrepreneurial ventures in times of change, so the street-smart business person stays on top of those things by doing everything possible to be informed, primed, and ready to act. It's a whole lot better to be the leader than a follower. If you look at our success we have always been the first in our markets with fitness products. We came out with the Ab Scissor in 2003 when the abdominal market was flat, so to speak. Now there are two or three abdominal products out there in some way, shape, or form, but another fifty or sixty that have tested and failed.

When we do our product planning sessions, we basically sit down and look at what we've done most recently *that worked well*. Then we look for what's next. There are a finite number of body parts. We're always challenging ourselves to make our products better with the latest and greatest technologies.

After we had great success with our Total Body Trainer, we looked to develop a product that was more focused, to reach a new segment of the market. We realized that we hadn't had a product for the abs market since 1998. So that's where we looked for a fresh opportunity. We are always looking for new ideas and we always have things in the works. It's become a very organic process that we're hardly even conscious of anymore because we've been doing it so long. That's a good habit to develop because it helps keep you ahead of the trends and market shifts.

Street Smarts for Opportunities

Street-smart success comes quickest when you prepare yourself to spot and jump on opportunities that suit your own unique talents and interests. Let's take a look at what sort of "smarts" it takes to identify and make the most of opportunities matched to your interests and talents.

1. A WIDE-BAND NETWORK

I've never yet met a street-smart success who was a hermit. Nearly all of us are always plugged in to what's going on in the world around us. Success happens when preparation meets opportunity. So, to prepare for street-smart success, you need a formal or informal system for processing potential opportunities and acting upon them.

> *I've never yet met a street-smart success who was a hermit.*

Most street-smart business wizards do this instinctively. It's just part of our gregarious personalities. We spend hours on the telephone every day keeping in touch with a network of business contacts, advisors, friends, lawyers, accountants, partners, employees, and even our competitors. We may not think of that network as a system for gathering opportunities, but that's how it works.

I have my own system, formed over the years of building businesses around my interests in the health and fitness fields. Most days when I'm not traveling, I don't go into my office in L.A. until late in the morning or early afternoon. But that doesn't mean I'm sleeping late or sitting at home eating bagels and cream cheese all morning. After my 5 A.M. workouts, I catch up on reading work-related documents. Most days I have breakfast with my wife Tracey and the kideroos, after which I hit my home office. There, I read the "trade" newspapers for each of my businesses, ranging from the *Hollywood Reporter* to *Sports Business Journal*. I take a quick look at a couple major newspapers to make sure I know what is going on in the world—keeping an eye out for anything that offers opportunities in the health and fitness fields.

And finally, I start dialing for dollars, baby. Well, not just dollars, but you might be amazed how many profitable opportunities get stirred up just by plugging into my network of business contacts, advisors, and street-smart friends. Opportunity works like electricity. You've got to be plugged in to get the charge. Information is the AC-DC current of opportunity. When information flows, so do opportunities. To know what the market wants and where the opportunities lie, you've got to be connected to a wide variety of information sources. Newspapers, trade magazines, the Internet, and your own network of personal contacts are invaluable and necessary sources of information.

> *Opportunity works like electricity. You've got to be plugged in to get the charge.*

The information current flows both ways. Not only do you have to gather and process information when looking for opportunities, you have to put it out there too. When I first began talking with the Seattle Seahawks about creating a Major League Lacrosse franchise in Seattle, I got to know their CEO, Tod Leiweke, who is a real community leader and just a great guy. He and I were having dinner in Seattle one night. I'd told Tod about meeting Starbucks founder Howard Schultz, who is also based in Seattle, and Tod noted that they'd never met. A few minutes later, Howard walked into the restaurant!

I introduced him to Tod and jokingly said, "How come you two aren't doing business together?" They laughed, but the next thing I knew, Tod was inviting Howard and his son, an avid Seahawks fan, to be his guests at their next NFL game. Later, both Tod and Howard thanked me for helping them connect. Who knows what will come of it? But my guess is that, at the very least, these two Seattle guys will become friends, and I'm proud to be the guy who hooked them up.

2. AN ALL-PLAY ATTITUDE

Street-smart successes don't believe in the old saying, "All work and no play makes Jack a dull boy." We have our own take on that: "If your work and your play aren't the same, you don't know Jack!" Or Jake!

Forget the work ethic; I'm an advocate of a strong play ethic. But that's because my work and my play are the same. It's not that I don't know how to relax. I can take a vacation with the best of them! But my work is my play, and I've found that it's the same for most street-smart successes. To an outsider, it might look like we're working hard, but we feel like we're playing hard because we love what we do and we do what we love.

There's a big payoff in having that attitude and living that lifestyle. The people who work with me at *Body By Jake* and at Major League Lacrosse often make comments about my high level of energy and the fact that I am always psyched up about what we do at those businesses. Since I'm a health and fitness guy, it's natural for them to assume that my super nova energy level comes from being in great physical shape. Well, it's true! But, it's also true that I get such a kick out of doing what I do that I'd crawl into the office every day if I had to.

| *For most street-smart successes, their work is their play.*

I'm going to say this in many different ways throughout this book because I think it is so important: You shouldn't think about pursuing street-smart success as building a business or a career. You should think about it as building a life! You should make your living with a sense of passion for what you do and a real hunger for the opportunities that are out there.

One of the greatest rewards that have come to me from having my own businesses and being an entrepreneur is that I never, ever get up in the morning and think, "Oh, I don't want to work today!" That's true because what I do isn't work. It's fun. And it's exciting because fresh opportunities crop up nearly every day. It's also fulfilling because the products we sell and the sport we promote are positive, beneficial, and enjoyable for our customers and our fans. I really believe that everyone involved in my enterprises—from the employees, to our partners, suppliers, advertisers, sponsors, players, customers, and fans—comes out a winner. And that's just a great way to live.

| *I never, ever get up in the morning and think, "Oh, I don't want to work today!"*

Most street-smart successes will tell you, profits come when you provide value to people—and that's what we're doing. I know it's true because one of the really interesting things about doing live television on the Home Shopping Network is that we take calls from viewers who've bought our products. We don't pay them to call in when we are on the air. We don't even know who is going to call or if anyone is going to call. But it never fails that one or two or sometimes five or six people call to talk about the value they've gotten from our products.

We have never scripted one of those calls and, to tell you the truth, most of them are so much better than I could ever dream up. Every now and then, we get worried because the callers praise our products so much that we're afraid people won't believe that it's an actual real-life customer. We had a caller to one HSN show who said she weighed more than the recommended maximum weight for the Ab Scissor. She was so excited because before ordering the product she was extremely depressed because of her weight. But after watching my show, she decided to make an effort to change her life. She thanked me and her whole family thanked me. Those are the moments that make everything we do worthwhile!

So, that's the secret of this street-smart success's high level of energy. When we get spontaneous calls from people who feel we've helped make their lives better, or when people stop me in airports to tell me that one of our products really worked for them, it pumps me up more than a week of workouts at the gym. When I see families having fun, cheering and enjoying great athletes performing in a true American sport at our Major League Lacrosse games, I feel like we've created something that contributes to the quality of life in this country. Who needs an energy drink when you can get a buzz like that? No wonder I'm always psyched up about new opportunities.

> *Your darkest days as an entrepreneur will be brighter than your brightest days of contributing to someone else's dreams!*

One more time then: Build your life around something that pumps you up too! Do something that makes *you* want to jump out of bed and go to work everyday. I promise you this, there will be tough days even when you love what you do. There will be disappointments. There will be setbacks and failures and stormy times. But your darkest days as an entrepreneur will be brighter than your brightest days of contributing to someone else's dreams!

3. A MAKE-IT-HAPPEN MODE

After reading the article on the lacrosse guy David Morrow that day on the plane, I began to develop the concept of Major League Lacrosse. It didn't take shape immediately as a formal a step-by-step plan, but some preliminary moves became obvious right away. First of all, I had to meet the man himself. He was obviously on the cutting edge of the sport, and I wanted to see what he thought of my idea. Like most street-smart successes, once I see a business opportunity and decide that it fits my talents and interests, I kick into a *make-it-happen mode*. I don't believe in letting ideas die as dreams. I believe in dreaming it and doing it! I set the bar higher because opportunities light my fire. They trigger my inner motivations to make a mark in this world by building things that last beyond my time on this planet. (Which I expect to be a long, long, long time, mind you.)

When I spot an opportunity that matches up with my interests, I become unstoppable. Other people may scoff, tell me I'm crazy, and tell me flat out that I'd be better off throwing my money down a sinkhole, but I don't see the problems that they see, I focus on solutions instead. And that is very typical of street-smart successes. Almost all of them are "can do" kind of people.

Do you know what a *Seabee* is? The Seabees are members of the U.S. Navy, but they pride themselves on being as tough as U.S. Marines and as resourceful as backwoods survivalists. The Seabees were created at the start of World War II as a new military breed, the fighting engineers and builders. Their job was to cut roads out of jungle in the Pacific, build bridges and even entire military bases and landing fields on mountaintops. Originally, the military had hired civilians to do the heavy lifting with those construction projects, but they proved to be easy targets for snipers and enemy soldiers because they weren't trained to fight. So, the military began recruiting tough construction workers, highway pavers, bridge builders, iron and sheet metal workers, and engineers, who were then sent through Marine boot camp. The members of the Construction Brigade, or CBs, became known as Seabees, who not only could fight but could also get things done under "impossible" circumstances. There was even a movie, *The Fighting Seabees*, starring John Wayne, the Duke himself.

The Seabees, who played a big role in toppling Saddam Hussein's dictatorship in Iraq, have an unofficial motto that reflects their spirit. It's "*Can do*." When given an assignment to do what others might think of as impossible, they pride themselves on responding, "Can do!" and then doing whatever it takes to get the job done. Street-smart successes have that same make-it-happen mode. We're Can-Do people too.

It's not that we just ignore challenges. We don't work with blinders on. But we focus on solutions rather than problems. We are tone deaf within the decibel range that includes phrases like "It can't be done" or "You'll never pull it off." I've never met a street-smart success who was a pessimist either. None of them have ever seen a glass of water as half empty. It's always half full. With few exceptions, we are people who came to believe in our ability to get things done very early in life.

> *Street-smart successes have never seen a glass of water as half empty. It's always half full.*

In my case, it was junior high. Once I began lifting weights, I learned that I could control what my body looked like, which eventually grew into the sense that it was always in my power to control my own happiness. Like most street-smart successes, I know I don't have power over what happens to me, so I focus on those things that I can control. When you have that sort of make-it-happen mode and Can-Do attitude, you learn to get around challenges and obstacles by shifting your focus to those areas that are within your power to deal with.

After reading the article on Warrior Lacrosse and its founder, I was pumped up. At the first opportunity, I tracked down his phone number and called David Morrow, but at first he wouldn't return my calls because he thought some of his old lacrosse buddies were "punking" him by pretending to be *Body By Jake*. When I finally did get him on the phone, it didn't take long for us to bond.

In my first conversation with him I only had two questions.

"David, is there such a thing as professional outdoor lacrosse?"

"No."

"Is there a governing body for the outdoor game?"

"No."

"Well, there is now, buddy."

As you can see, I was already in the make-it-happen mode. I'm not going to tell you that building a professional sports league from scratch is an easy thing to do. Sure, there have been times when I felt like a Seabee trying to build a landing strip in a jungle on top of a mountain during monsoon season. But if street-smart success was easy, what fun would it be? We'd all be rich. The country clubs would be full. And we'd be stuck playing golf every day of the week.

The fact is that there are very few truly original business ideas out there. I'm sure that somewhere there are other people who at some point had their own ideas about home lap pools or gourmet cookies or personal devices for downloading music off the Internet. But an opportunity is only an idea or a dream until someone with a make-it-happen, Can-Do attitude snatches it up.

Street-smart success comes to those who not only see opportunities but take action on them. Some describe that initiative as a competitive drive. Others say it's a sense of urgency, a desire for accomplishment, creative expression, or a restless energy. Every street-smart success I know has it in one form or another. We all want to make a mark. We want to leave something behind. We want to build something bigger, stronger, or faster that will make the world a little better. So we create or track down opportunities, jump on them, and do everything in our power to transform them from dreams to reality.

> *Street-smart success comes to those who not only see opportunities but take action on them.*

Once I talked to Dave Morrow, I knew that there was an opportunity waiting for action in my idea for a professional outdoor lacrosse league. At that point, all I had invested in that idea was a 5-cents-a-minute long-distance phone call. When I hung up the phone in 1998, the opportunity was still hanging there like something said after the connection was lost. It was nothing more than a thought floating on air. As I write this six years later, Major League Lacrosse is a reality in Baltimore, Rochester, New Jersey, Boston, Long Island, and Philadelphia. It's a reality for hundreds of players, team officials, fans, and sponsors. And it's become the fastest growing game in the country, as more and more people are seeing more and more opportunities within it.

How did that happen? Why did it happen? What made it happen? Was it initiative? Creative expression? Restless energy? A sense of urgency? Probably all of those in varying degrees. Major League Lacrosse is the result of opportunity inspiring action. The idea inspired by the magazine article was like a match that hadn't been struck until I got things moving, but once I did, the flame spread rapidly. Street-smart successes take the initiative on opportunities. They act as catalysts, bringing together ideas with actions. They gather financial resources with all of the other elements, including the real estate, the raw materials, the labor, the manufacturing, and the delivery services.

We'll take a look at all of those steps later, but for now it's important to take a look inside yourself. If it's really your dream to be a street-smart success, you'll have to have your own sources of internal motivation so that you'll be able to not only see opportunities but also to translate them into action. What gets you fired up? What motivates you to keep chasing your dream even when things aren't going your way? Is there a favorite saying? An inspirational story? The encouragement of a parent or other loved one?

Keep in mind that *negative sources can be turned into positive forces*! Did someone once tell you that you'd never amount to anything? That your dreams were beyond your reach? That you'd eat their dust? Everyone has rivals or competition or people who've put them down. Use those sources as positive forces too. You might want to make a list of your possible sources of motivation and inspiration right now. On the lines below write down your sources of inner motivation:

1. _____

2. _____

3. _____

4. _____

5. _____

Everyone has unique sources of motivation. I've known some very successful people who've motivated themselves to reach high levels of achievement simply by deciding that they were going to prove enemies or critics wrong. So, don't feel bad if that's one source of motivation for you. I would discourage you from using money or wealth or material things as motivational sources to drive your search for opportunities. A Mercedes-Benz is a nice reward for being successful but it's not a worthy source of motivation because once you've got a garage full of Benzes you will still need something to get you pumped up. So look at that list for your own inner sources of motivation and learn to tap into them so that you'll always be ready when opportunities for street-smart success appear.

If you believe it, you will achieve it!

getting into the game

I'M NOT GOING to pretend that I grew up wanting to be an entrepreneur. I wasn't that street smart myself. I got into business doing what came naturally. People saw I was fit, so they asked me to help them get in shape. I was in Hollywood, so many of those people were entertainers, producers and directors. All kinds of trends begin in California, and I'm proud to have been the guy behind one of them. Personal fitness training began with me and my clients. It was an accidental career, so I didn't have a business plan or any kind of plan at all when that operation took off.

One day I was just guy trying to make it as a bodybuilder in Southern California. The next thing I knew, I had the hottest, sweatiest boutique business in Hollywood. That's what happens when you jump on an opportunity that matches perfectly with your interests. It's magical!

When word started getting around Hollywood that Jake was the guy who could get stars in great shape, the world beat a path to my door. I had reporters from *People* magazine and scores of others hunting me down for a story. The headlines! The paparazzi! The people I owed money to who suddenly thought I was rich . . . oy vey! Naw, just kidding. It was fan-tastic!

> *You can have a kicking concept for your business, but without a rock-'em, sock-'em business plan, you'll never be a contender.*

The whole concept of a personal fitness trainer was so pure and perfect for Hollywood that the business took off on its own. And that was fine at first because it was just me and my gear back then. But if your street-smart business is going to be any bigger than one man, one broom, one towel, and one chair, you need a plan, Stan.

A business plan is, for all intents and purposes, a road map. Now, I know, some people think it's not cool to have a map or ask directions. But we're not talking about a trip to Disneyland here. This is your business and your life! So get with it. You can have great goals and a wonderful concept for your business, but without a well-done business plan, you're going nowhere fast.

A good business plan serves as your map for starting, developing, and growing your business but it's much more than that. It is also the showpiece document you present to bankers, potential investors, and suppliers to let them know that you're not just playing around with the idea of starting your own business. Notice, though, that I said a *good* business plan. Any banker or venture capitalist can tell horror stories about being approached by aspiring entrepreneurs whose business plans look like they were submitted for a third grade coloring contest.

It's true that Southwest Airlines, the nation's most profitable commercial passenger service, began with a business plan written on a napkin—but that isn't what the original investors were given. I'm sure there are some ideas that are so brilliant that their street-smart creators have gotten millions from bankers with business plans written on the back of cocktail napkins. But chances are, your concept may need a bit more razzamatazz, or at least a better stock of paper and ink.

In most cases, the quality of your business plan communicates the quality of your idea and serves as evidence that you have the moxie to make it happen. It is a reflection of just how serious, how committed, and how prepared you are to not only get it up and running but to keep the doors open through those crucial first six months when the great majority of new businesses do the big nose dive.

| *Make sure you can deliver on the promises of your plan!*

Your business plan is not a wish list. It is supported by serious research and thought. It should get you through at least the first six months of operation with only minor adjustments. And if done in a professional manner, it will not only define your business concept and lure investors, it will also help in the launch of your product or services, while providing a careful evaluation of the competition and market to minimize risks.

Remember, the worst thing you can do in a business plan, or as a business person in general, is to over-promise and under-deliver. Instead, you should make it a point in the plan and in your daily business to under-promise and over-deliver!

By now, you are probably catching my drift. You've got to take the time to do this right. You'll be asking serious people to give you serious dough based on your business plan, so this is not the time to cut corners or toss off something during commercials. Having a professional, well-done business plan may mean the difference between getting or not getting your vital start-up loan and a line of credit at the bank. It can win over skeptics and doubters. But if it looks like a community-college theme paper, you might as well stand on a street corner and panhandle for pennies.

Consider Your Audience

Before you even start working on your business plan you should think a bit about your reading audience. Your buddies and best friends may buy into your business idea based on your enthusiasm, brilliance, and willingness to pay the bar tab, but bankers and venture capitalists don't invest in good will. If the figures don't add up, they won't step up. They will want to know your company's fixed assets, including buildings and equipment.

Bankers and most other potential investors will want to feel assured that you are capable of repaying any loans at the going interest rate. Unlike loan sharks, bankers won't threaten to take out your knee caps if you default on the loan, but they could take your house, your car, and your reputation if you aren't careful in structuring your deal with them. If money matters aren't your thing, don't try to fake it. Most business operators weren't finance majors. It might be a good idea to ask a friend or a professional you know with experience in banking and finance to work with you as a consultant on your business plan, either for a fee or—careful here—for a percentage of the profits or loan received.

> *It pays to make sure the financial figures for your plan add up.*

Putting a solid plan together involves some serious getting-down-to-business, but you'll be glad you invested the time, energy, and calculator batteries. A good business plan pays off many times during the early years of your business and for years after. It puts on paper both the dreams and the realities of your business. You may well make adjustments, fine-tune, and even radically change your business plan over the years, but it always serves as a road map that you can check when you feel like it's straying off course. With Major League Lacrosse we've revamped the business plan every other week or so. That's what street-smart entrepreneurs do!

Once *Body By Jake* became a business with employees and licensed products, of course, we created a business plan that we have followed and adjusted over the years. So, when I saw the opportunity to develop Major League Lacrosse, we pulled out the *Body By Jake* business plan. And guess what? I quickly saw that MLL needed its own plan. It was simply a different type of business concept. Was I upset about that? Not in any way shape or form. You see, that's what a well-crafted business plan is supposed to do. It should tell you when your businesses need to be closely linked and when they need to be independent of each other.

> *Make sure your new business fits the mix.*

Even though I saw that Major League Lacrosse would help bring a younger demographic group to the *Body By Jake* brand, it was set up as a separate entity. I took measures to be certain that the new venture, which carried higher risks, didn't in any way threaten the very good thing we had going with our core business. That's something to keep in mind if you start more than one business, which is pretty typical of street-smart successes. You don't want to burden the finances, or the personnel, of your successful operations with the growing pains of start up enterprises, especially if there aren't a lot of synergies with your existing businesses. It can be cost-effective to centralize and consolidate areas like payroll, benefits, and purchasing if you have several businesses. But if there is really no synergy between a new enterprise and your other operations, the apple and oranges rule applies. It's best to keep them separate.

Defining Your Successful Business

The good news is that you don't have to have a Harvard MBA to put together a good business plan. There are many Web sites that offer templates and forms for creating a business plan so you can get the basics there. I have my own special twists on the standard format, so let's look at the essential elements of a street-smart business plan.

THE EXECUTIVE SUMMARY

I've put together and presented a lot of business plans over the years and I'm not kidding you when I tell you that this is *the* most important section of your plan. Why? Because a high percentage of people who read your plan will look at this first. If they like what they see, they'll keep reading. If they don't, kiss them goodbye. That's why you want to write this section *last*, after you've seen how all of the other aspects come together. It's called the summary because it offers a brief nutshell look at what's in the rest of the plan, which includes:

- The nuts-and-bolts details of your business concept and a brief history of how you came up with it.

- A market overview.

- An in-depth look at the competition.

- A serious analysis of your customers or clients.

- A no-bull presentation of your product or service and its unique aspects.

- Your money needs to start up, and to keep going, for the first three, five, and ten years.

- Projections for growth and return on investment over those same time periods.

- Any major achievements or developments within the business or its target market that are vital to success. This could include everything from getting a patent approved, copyrighting original material, winning a lawsuit, getting zoning approval, completing a prototype, or winning a big government or private contract.

You shouldn't write your executive summary until you have all the other sections at least roughed out, just to make certain that you've got all your ducks in a row. But there are some things to keep in mind for the executive summary while you are writing the rest of your business plan.

- *Don't fudge the numbers, even a little.* Sure, it's tempting to project your dreams of huge sales and great earnings when writing the business plan. And you'll probably be tempted to ask for a lot more money than you need because you believe that your business will take off like gangbusters from the get-go. After all, street-smart successes are optimistic, can-do kind of people right? Well, the problem is that bankers, investors and other money-minded folks aren't buying into your dreams, they are investing—or not investing—in the realities of your business plan. So go by the numbers. Base your calculations on realistic measures and stick with figures that don't lie. You'll be dealing with experienced accountants, bankers, and business people who won't be easily fooled anyway, so you might as well work on building up your reputation as a straight-shooter.

| *Don't try to sell your dreams. Sell the power of your plan.*

- *Skip the rockets' red glare and bombs bursting in air.* There will be plenty of sales presentations down the road. Your business plan is not the place to make a pitch. While it is important to show enthusiasm and to present a strong case as to why you think your business concept will work, your business plan should be pretty straightforward in laying out the facts. So keep the bells and whistles to a minimum. That means you'll probably have to save the chorus line and the sky-writing for the first big meeting with advertisers or sales managers.

■ *Make a long story short.* Some very busy people who are fully capable of billing clients thousands of dollars per hour will be spending their valuable time reading your business plan. They'll scan the executive summary first to see if it catches their interest. It should be only two or three pages long and filled with hard information. So don't waste it on adjectives, cute stories about your five-year old, or technical jargon designed to impress your advanced-computer-physics professor. Look at it this way: The quicker they get through your business plan, the faster they can make a decision to give you the money.

■ *Don't leave out anything important.* Give yourself at least six months to put your business plan together so that you have time to think about all aspects of what you'll be doing, producing, offering, selling, and delivering. Talk it through with family members and experienced business people you trust. Listen to their questions, because the things they want to know will probably reflect what bankers, potential investors, partners, suppliers, and customers will want to see in the plan.

■ *Tell them what makes your business unique.* Anything that makes your product or service stand out from the crowd and the competition is really important. Professional money lenders sniff this out because if there is truly something special about your company, like a secret recipe, a new formula, a money-back guarantee, or a ground-breaking technology, it gives them all the more reason for buying into your plan.

So, if your swimming pools are small enough to fit in the guest room, that's worth noting. If your commuter car runs on morning dew and hits speeds of 110 miles per hour, that's important too. Make sure you present the unique aspects of your product that will make it shine in the marketplace. Don't be afraid to specifically say how your product or service will stand out against your biggest competitors. If your Exit signs shine brighter and give off beeps during power failures compared to the non-beeping competition, make that point. If your Italian restaurant has 10,000 more bottles in its wine cellar and a much better calamari recipe than the joint down the street, let 'em know that too.

▪ *If there is some realistic and compelling evidence that your business concept is going to change the world, create a revolution in its field, or otherwise upset the balance of the universe, put it in this section.* But make sure you know what you are talking about. It wouldn't hurt to have a trusted advisor, local professors, or successful uncle entrepreneur read over your Summary before you pass it around just to make sure you don't make some foolish mistake.

Get It Out of Your Head and on Paper

Most street-smart entrepreneurs are big dreamers who think about business opportunities night and day. Once I've got an idea in my head, the wheels start churning constantly. I may be doing other things, but I'm also thinking about how I can make the new idea work, the people I want to get involved, the contacts I'll need to make, and how I'll fund the start up and then keep it going for the first year and on down the road. That's a lot to keep banging around in my brain, so when my head starts to hurt, I'll begin putting it down on paper. It helps me to see things more clearly, plus there's just something about putting it in writing that makes it seem more real. Let's take a look at the other basic elements that need to go into your business plan.

COMPANY SUMMARY

This is the meet-n'-greet section in which you introduce yourself, your top ranked employees, and your business. Include brief biographies of yourself and other top executives, and a brief history of your business concept telling how the idea was formed. If you find yourself beginning: "I was born . . ." you probably want to flash ahead a couple decades. Again, the people who will be reading this are very busy and you want them to be in a good and generous mood when they finish. They don't care that you walked before your cousins crawled, okay?

PRODUCT AND SERVICE ANALYSIS

This is where you lay out what will make your product or service stand out from the competition. You don't want to turn this into a dog-and-pony pitch.

Offer a straight-up report on why you think there is a place in the market for your business idea. Give a summary paragraph describing the value or benefits that will be provided to your target market by your product or service. You should also include the location or locations you've chosen and why they are important, the key technologies involved, a detailed description of your product or services, and potential future products or services.

If your Yoga N' Yogurt Shoppe is designed to be the first in a nationwide chain, put that down on paper. If your Internet Anywhere service will beam the World Wide Web into every home in the nation through the plumbing fixtures, let it flow. Don't embellish on the facts, but do lay it out for them.

MARKET ANALYSIS

This is where the rubber meets the road. Two out of three new businesses fail within five years. The primary reason for failure by start-up businesses is a lack of in-depth market analysis before the "Open for Business" sign goes up in the window. You can't just assume that the world is going to flock to your door. Well, I guess you can assume that if you are financing your own business with cash or your lottery winnings and you have an "easy come, easy go" philosophy. But if you are borrowing money from a bank, depending on outside investors, or hoping to build your life around this business, you'll need to do your market research homework. Now, don't get nervous here. It's a whole lot better knowing you studied for the test so you can sleep on it and whiz through it. But don't make yourself nuts.

| *Make sure you know the market before you open shop.*

If you have to hire a professional market analysis company to do it for you, spend the money. In this section, you should include analysis of the industry you'll be involved in, its historical cycles, and future forecasts. Your market analysis should include a list of all known competitors, with descriptions of their products, market share, profitability, and any competitive edge or deficit that relates to your proposed business. You should also offer an explanation as to how your product matches up in competition with theirs.

Trade-association Web sites and periodicals are great sources of information for collecting this sort of market intelligence. Most trade groups are more than happy to provide you with information if they think you may be a member someday. Check out resources and Web sites like the *Encyclopedia of Associations,* the *Thomas Register of Manufacturers,* and the *Rand McNally Commercial Atlas and Marketing Guide*, among others.

STRATEGIC PLAN

This is where the action is. Once you've laid out what your product or services are, who the players will be, and where the "battle" will take place, it's time for the war plan. This section of your business plan should cover your pricing strategies, marketing plans, distribution channels, sales strategies, promotion efforts and forecasts for the next three to five years. These should be highly detailed to illustrate that you've done your homework. For example, you should separate your total sales by product or department line so that you'll be able to spot trends and seasonal shifts. (Don't you love it when I get down to business like that?)

MANAGEMENT PROFILE

Earlier in the Company Summary section, you provided brief biographies of yourself and your top executives. In this section, you go into much more depth by including biographies of department heads and other key players, particularly those with great credentials, awards, or high profiles in your field or industry. Keep in mind that many potential investors and bankers may be more interested in who is on your team than in what you are selling. Investors are very interested in the management. It is super important, and as much of a genius as you may be, you gotta have a good team around. Otherwise, you may just be a legend in your own shower.

List every individual's undergraduate and graduate degrees, work experience, awards, and any other vital information you'd want to know if you were a potential investor or banker looking at this startup company. Boy Scout badges and 4-H ribbons probably don't warrant mention.

| *A top-notch team is an asset you can sell to investors.*

Also in this section, include an organizational chart showing who reports to whom, with the job descriptions and duties of each and every employee.

It wouldn't hurt also to include your list of potential consultants, advisers, board directors, and professionals, like the lawyers, accountants, and technical experts who'll be called upon when needed.

Spend some time evaluating this section before you hand over your business plan to any outsiders, because it will give you an early overall view of your team. You might want to consider at this point whether there are any obvious weaknesses or missing pieces. Does your team have the up-to-date technical knowledge necessary? The sales experience? The marketing know-how? The industry expertise? The diversity demanded of a modern business?

Now is also a good time to look in the mirror. Do you have a good handle on your own strengths and weaknesses as a member of this team? Are there other team members whose strengths match up to your weaknesses? Are there executives on board who are willing to challenge you and to tell you the truth even if you may not want to hear it? We'll go into this more later, but you need to take this aspect of your business very seriously.

FINANCIAL ANALYSIS

I've already made the point that your motive for starting your business shouldn't be pure profit. You've got to live it every day so it had better be something you enjoy doing and take pride in being part of. Let's face it, one of the most profitable businesses out there is trash removal, but people aren't lining up to get into the industry. There are those in that line of work, however, who take pride in finding environmentally sound ways to dispose of garbage. I'm glad they are out there. And I have no problem that they are reaping the financial rewards of their work. Your business should reward you in both ways too.

In this section of the business plan, you dial up the dollars. Here, you lay out the proposed amounts and sources for:

- Start-up financing

- Operating funds

- Cash reserves

- Revolving credit

Bankers, potential investors and partners, and others who'll be reading your business plan also want to know the details of:

- Your business and personal assets

- Your business and personal debts

- Financial projections from your market research

- Projected equipment costs

- Projected supply costs

- Projected lease or mortgages costs

- Projected salary and benefit costs for all employees

- Projected manufacturing costs

- Projected delivery costs

- Projected costs of accounting, legal, and technological services

| *Play it straight all the way.*

This is another place where you don't want to play cute. Most serious investors and bankers have ways of accessing your personal and professional financial records, including your credit reports and public records of any civil or criminal cases you've been party to. So if there are skeletons in your closet, including bankruptcies or legal disputes with past business associates, customers, or suppliers, it would be wise to come clean voluntarily rather than being forced to cough up the information later. You're better off being up front with the information than risk looking like you attempted to hide something.

It's wise to keep in mind here that the people who will be reading your business plan likely have not just toppled off the old turnip truck. Assume that they've probably seen and heard it all. That could work in your favor in that most savvy bankers and investors understand that even the most honest people get sued or have legal disagreements with former associates. Even bankruptcies no longer leave the long term stain on reputations that they once did. But you should be prepared to answer any and all questions if you expect these people to invest their money or time in your business.

| *Sell what you've got, not what you hope to get.*

Keep in mind that it is standard practice that most start-up owners pad their financial needs by about 25 percent in their business plans. Remember too that any veteran investment pro or banker will automatically subtract about 25 percent for that very reason. They also know that you may try to impress them by overstating revenue projections. But most will be far more interested in how you plan on making money than on how much money you think you may be pulling in. When you write this section of the business plan, follow the philosophy of impressing them with what you know and understand about your business rather than with what you hope it will produce down the road.

But wait! There's more!

Your future investors and bankers will want to see a break-even analysis with your projections of how much money you will have to put out before your business starts turning a profit. Hint: This analysis should *never* include the following terms:

Money pit

Black hole

Lost cause

Titanic

It *should* include a balance sheet showing assets, liabilities, and equity for each quarter over the next three to five years. Also do a cash flow schedule showing how cash will be spent and collected over the same period.

If you are buying an existing business, your investors and bankers will want to see a balance sheet showing the company's assets, liabilities, and equity ownership. There should also be a profit and loss statement. This should reflect the results of operations by comparing total revenues against all operating costs—expenses such as supplies, salaries, insurance, and any other overhead—not including the Jacuzzi in your office. But nice try anyway.

Plans for existing and start-up businesses should include cash-flow forecasts tracking the flow of income and expenditures so that your potential investors or bankers can calculate how much money or credit will be needed to keep your business buoyant. Also required is a break-even analysis that shows how long it will take a business to turn a profit. That point is usually reached when sales revenues equal total costs.

The Executive Summary Revisited

Once you've completed all of these sections of the business plan, you are ready to go back and do your executive summary. Take your time and do it right. If you weren't exactly the star of your English composition class, ask for help from a writerly friend.

Here are key things to keep in mind when writing your business plan.

1. DON'T FARM IT OUT

It's okay to get help in certain areas where expertise is needed, like the financial nuts and bolts, but the business plan is something you should and must do yourself. You need to know your venture inside out, and your business plan is one of the most critical aspects of any operation. If you aren't interested enough to do the business plan yourself, then it's very likely you are in the wrong business. Writing a business plan forces you to look at all aspects of the operation. Any flaws in your strategy or financial projections will show up here if you do your homework.

It could well be that in doing the business plan you may lose your enthusiasm for this business concept. That's not such a bad deal. It's better that you bail out before you've committed resources and other people have signed on or loaned you money. If doing the business plan only pumps you up more about the concept, that's great! Writing a business plan is hard work but if you get through it and you are still enthused about the idea, then you are probably on the right track.

| *Check your heart while writing your plan.*

2. CHECK IT. CHECK IT AGAIN. CHECK YOUR CHECKS

Have somebody else double-check it too. While you are doing the business plan, make sure you keep track of all of your sources of information and hold on to them in case you need to verify something later on. Go over it when you are done and check all the math, the spelling, and the punctuation. You can be sure that some of the people who read your business plan will be nit-pickers. That's what they are paid to be. If they see a sloppy business plan, they'll likely think you'll be sloppy in your business dealings. That can be a deal killer.

If you've included graphs and charts or a power point presentation as part of the plan, check and double-check them too. It's often easy to miss mistakes in that type of material, so print it out and eyeball it. And finally, look up the high school English teacher who nearly flunked you for not crossing a "t" or not dotting an "i," and have her go over it too. By the way, get in the habit of being this careful about everything you do in your business. Later on, even little mistakes can cost you big bucks.

3. GET PUMPED AND GET TOUGH!

You might want to stock up on deodorant and antiperspirant because the bankers and venture capital folks want to see you sweat. Not all of them are *that* bad, I'm told, and in truth, they're probably doing you a favor by putting you through the wringer. They want to make sure you know your business inside out, upside down, and sideways, and they need to know that if they commit their money, you will be committed to making your business work. You can't go into a business plan presentation half-heartedly. This is a sales pitch. You've got to be pumped up so you can pump them up. If that means stopping by Starbucks and downing a triple espresso, then do it. But be prepared for the grilling.

Make a trial run or two with friends who are good at playing bad guys. Have them put you through the third degree. Maybe you should look up a business professor or a banker friend of the family and do a practice run. Do whatever it takes to get ready, because these are critical meetings for you and the future of your street-smart success.

4. ANALYZE YOUR AUDIENCE

You may be presenting your business plan to a variety of people, including bankers, venture capitalists, family investors, acquaintances with an interest in investing, potential board members, management or employee candidates and possible partners, suppliers, or distributors. You'll want all of them to buy into your concept, but you should customize your pitch for each of them. If possible, do some homework on the interests and backgrounds of each group. One venture capitalist, for example, might have a special interest in high-tech companies while another might prefer home products. An older family member might be more interested in a short-term return than a younger family member who is looking for long-term investments.

Know the needs of your market.

It's also true that your line of work, where your business is located, and other factors will play into the pitch presentation. You need to understand the needs of every person you are addressing and then design your presentation accordingly. Bankers and venture capitalists will be particularly interested in your financial data and your financial resources. Family members interested in investing in your business will want to know that the kid who put a carton of Jell-O mix in the neighbor's garden fountain is now serious about building a business. Prospective board members and employees will want to know about the benefits and salaries and the long-term plans for your business.

Also, your audience might expect a young entrepreneur involved in an Internet start-up or a video-game software company to be dressed in a hipper style than a woman starting a home nursing care service. But again, no matter what business you are in, you will be expected to make a professional and accurate presentation of your proposed business, which means you'd better know your audience. This is a lesson I learned the hard way. You might say it was a "cereal" killer.

When Tim Robertson and I were on the road pitching advertisers for commercial time for my *Big Brother Jake* show on the Family Channel, we went to General Mills, the cereal company. I was talking to their advertising buyers about how great a family show it would be for them to advertise on. I even suggested that we'd put their cereals right on the kitchen table during the show. Their eyes lit up at that. I was on a roll! But then I rolled over the edge.

I got off on this thing about how we only did responsible family programming that promoted wholesome and healthy lifestyles—just like General Mills. It had clicked in my mind that General Mills made Wheaties, so I got on a tangent how we'd never show kids eating cereals that are laced with sugar, but instead we'd feature healthy General Mills cereals like Wheaties, the breakfast of Champions!

It was about this point that Tim began kicking my legs under the table. I was so pumped up, I thought he was urging me to keep talking about sugar-free cereal, so I laid it on thicker, talking about how responsible General Mills was for promoting cereals like Cheerios and Wheaties. When the meeting came to an end, I thought I'd nailed the presentation. I was expecting the General Mills media buyers to offer us a multi-million dollar contract right there. Instead, they thanked us very politely and said they'd be in touch.

Once we were outside the building, Tim clued me in.

"I was kicking you to get you to shut up about sugar free cereals!" he said.

"What? Aren't these the Wheaties guys?" I asked.

"Yes, and they are also the Cocoa Puffs, Count Chocula, and Lucky Charms guys! Didn't you see their posters on the wall?"

"No, I guess I missed them," I replied.

We also missed out on getting any advertising from General Mills, simply because I didn't know my audience!

5. KEEP IT CONFIDENTIAL

In an ideal world, you could pitch your business plan without every worrying that someone in the audience with more money or better connections might steal the idea and get a business up and running before you get yours out of the blocks. But that ideal world doesn't exist, unfortunately. People talk. And they steal. Sometimes it's just a conversational slip about this "great idea" that someone else takes and runs with. I'm afraid it happens all the time.

To prevent it from happening to you and your inspired business idea, do the street-smart thing and get a lawyer to draft a confidentiality agreement. Before you present your business plan to anyone, discretely ask that each person in the room sign a copy of that agreement. Don't worry, professionals and people who really care about you and your success will understand, and they'll appreciate that you are being careful and thorough in protecting your business concept. Anyone who balks at signing it can take a hike. You don't want to do business with them anyway.

| *Protect your plan with confidentiality agreements.*

6. KEEP IT CURRENT

Even after you've landed financing and launched the business, it's wise to check in with your business plan on a regular basis; if not every quarter, at least every six months to a year. Your target market may shift. The economy may rise or fall. New technologies may come along. So, you need to make adjustments and fine-tune your business plan accordingly. One simple shift in your day-to-day practices can affect the entire operation.

Let's say you just stumbled across an incredibly talented and energetic person whose skills are desperately needed, and so you hire this prized catch on the spot. An unplanned new hire like that will impact everything from your company's weekly payroll and its health and benefits funds, to office space and future earnings. So you've got to get into the plan and do some fast footwork.

It's also a good idea to go into your plan on a regular basis just to check your budget against actual performance and to make an honest and detailed long-term review of your business. You may discover that you've been keeping too much excess inventory, or that supply costs have crept up, or that your profit forecasts were way too pessimistic (yeah, baby!). Most companies are organic operations that develop new revenue streams, discard products that don't work, and shed and add employees over time. That's a good thing—as long as you stay on top of the constant change by adjusting your plan as you go.

It's Good for You!

Doing a business plan is like eating your veggies. You may not enjoy it but it is good for you and for your business. Make it as enjoyable as you can by understanding that this one big step will carry you a long way in the process of starting, financing and growing your business. Once you've got a solid business plan together, you are on your way to street-smart success! So, hunker down, do it right, and know that you are taking a big step on the path to your dreams as an entrepreneur!

| *Be ready to move and groove.*

Understand that your business plan will always change. It may even become an entirely different business. You've got to be ready to move and groove! Be willing to go with Plan B, C, and D so that you can adjust to new developments and circumstances. Business plans are made to be changed!

4

put together your team

STREET-SMART SUCCESSES are independent, self-motivated, and self-confident people. But believe me, they aren't Lone Rangers when it comes to doing business. You are going to need help.

To get your business up and running and to keep it going for the short and long haul, you are going to need people whose skills, knowledge, and expertise builds upon yours. It's important that you learn all you can about your business. But you've got to know your limitations too.

We are social animals for a very basic reason: survival. We have survived as a species because we work together to help each other overcome obstacles and withstand the challenges of life, whether it's a Tyrannosaurus Rex looking for lunch, or a competing company stalking your customers.

| Teamwork works!

From a Hollywood perspective, I've seen a lot of famous people whose only product was themselves. Yet, each and every one of them depended on a trusted team. Every actor and actress depends on agents, managers, lawyers, accountants, public relations people, makeup experts, wardrobe aces, fitness trainers—especially fitness trainers—and others to keep their careers on track.

No matter how street smart you may be, you probably can't do it all, know it all, or see it all. To ensure the long-term survival and success of your business endeavors, you need to put together a team whose strengths and perspectives complement and build upon your own. So let's take a look at what sort of team you might need for your business, and how to get the best and the brightest, and most trustworthy people on your side. Your "team" should include:

1. Business partners

2. Employees

3. A trusted "cabinet" of wise advisors or a board of directors

4. A wide network of business and personal associates who share information and connections to help each other

5. Go-to guys—your most trusted friends and family members

Partnering Up

In 1983, I started doing the *Fitness Break by Jake* for viewers on Cable News Network (CNN). After four years and more than 800 vignettes, I ran out of things to do with a broomstick, towel, and chair, and so I started calling fitness equipment companies to see if I could get props to pump up the show. I needed to find a source to loan or give me fitness equipment because I didn't have an equipment budget for the CNN spots. I was hoping to get a "permanent loan" of the equipment because my friends, Richard and Judy Friedman, had been letting me shoot the CNN spots at their beautiful Beverly Hills home and I had told them that I'd return the favor by getting some equipment for a home gym for them too.

I felt I had some leverage because my CNN spots were building my brand and I could offer an equipment maker exposure that was worth a lot of money. I went through the Yellow Pages, calling fitness equipment makers and pitching them on my free-products-for-television-time opportunity. I got all the way to the Ps before finding anyone willing to talk to me further. Polaris fitness equipment was top notch and their marketing vice president, Phil Scotti, seemed to think I was offering a fair trade. He didn't hang up on me like most of the other people I'd called. Instead, he said, "I'm in!" Within a short time, we cut a deal and he sent the equipment I needed to the Friedman's house.

Phil and I really hit it off. Over the weeks that followed we spent a lot of time talking. I told him that I was thinking big. I had a vision for my brand that went way beyond its origins. He had some great ideas of how to do that. I'd just begun to develop the *Body By Jake* brand around that time by doing endorsements for fitness equipment. Phil and I talked about the ins and outs of that.

We still laugh about one of my first endorsement deals, which I got before Phil came around. The product was an "exercise stick" that was basically a broomstick without the broom. It didn't take people long to figure out they could make their own. Let's just say its magical properties didn't exactly take the market by storm. I'd also done a fitness book and a video, and my business was really starting to take off.

Phil knew the fitness industry and, like me, he believed that there was a lot more I could be doing to tap into the rapidly growing market. I really liked that he bought into my vision for the company, and it got him excited too. Still, our partnership didn't happen overnight. We worked together for more than a year, talking about the possibilities and getting to know each other. The more we talked, the more we both got enthused about working together to develop the *Body By Jake* brand in the fitness industry. Finally, he left Polaris after twelve years to help me launch *Body By Jake* as a licensing company.

From the start, we've worked as a tag team, with Phil's strengths complementing mine. We're very different type guys and we have very different roles, but we respect and like each other and we work really well together. Phil's very detail oriented. He is great at product research and development and the nuts and bolts of all aspects of business. He didn't know much about television production in those early years but I taught him what I learned. Over the years, he has become a real genius at producing fitness programming, as well as overseeing budgets and other details.

I'm the gregarious guy in the front of the store, pulling people in off the street, always looking and cooking opportunities, making connections, and pushing everyone to get to the top. I'm the full-steam-ahead guy. Phil is the guy who wants to take it slow, see how much it's going to cost, and check things out before making the leap.

| Pick a partner you can live with.

We balance each other out, so we make a great team. We've had incredible successes that have earned us the respect of our industry, and a few buckaroos too. It hasn't always come easy. Early on, it was hard for me to give up control, even a little bit. But Phil is such an honest, straightforward guy that he won me over. I can easily overpower people with the constant flow of new ideas and propositions. Phil is no pushover either. He insists on making sure that all the t's are crossed and all the i's are dotted. The key is that we trust each other and we communicate openly. We both want the business to grow and prosper.

A business partnership is like a marriage. Once you've signed the agreement, you are stuck with each other for better or for worse, in good times and in bad, in sickness and in health, and in bankruptcy or financial success. So pick your partners carefully. Make certain that you respect each other and don't compete with each other. Understand that you will have your disagreements, so you'd better have a working relationship based on mutual trust.

I really appreciate Phil and the strength of our partnership because I had a business "marriage" go bad before we hooked up. My business in L.A. was really thriving and, as a native of Long Island, I wanted to make an impact in the Big Apple. (They tell me if you can make it there, you can make it anywhere!) I was looking for opportunities in New York, when I met an extremely bright and energetic woman who was running a successful chain of fitness studios in Manhattan. People had been encouraging me to open my own gym, and the thought of having one in New York City was really exciting. I talked with her about opening a *Body By Jake* studio there and she jumped at the opportunity to join me. It was my name on the door, and I was responsible for the financing. But, since she was going to be there day in and day out, I went along with her when she asked to be a full partner in the deal. We put together a solid business plan and started looking for a location.

To his credit, my attorney, Bob Lieberman, told me that I should not open a business that was going to be 3,000 miles away. He also felt that I needed to build a stronger infrastructure for my company before I started growing it in such an aggressive manner. Still, my optimistic, go-for-it attitude prevailed. It also won out when the space we leased turned out to be nearly four times the size we'd originally agreed upon—at quadruple the rent. We'd put together a sensible budget, planning to spend only $2000 a month on rent—this was back in the affordable 80s, mind you. But then, we saw a space in Midtown Manhattan and I got so fired up that we ended up spending $9000. What can I say; the thought of having a prime location in Manhattan got me excited!

The fitness studio business is a tough business, yet when it is done right, it generates rivers of cash. I wanted to make certain there was someone there I could count on to take care of salaries, bills, and taxes. My partner had all the skills and drive to make it work. Our New York fitness center was a hit from the day we opened the door for business. But then, my partner decided that since she was doing such a great job of running the place, she wanted her name on that door too. She wanted to become part of the *Body By Jake* brand. I don't blame her for trying, but that just wasn't going to happen.

My lawyer was right, even if it has taken me twenty-five years to admit it. Just kidding. I acknowledged his wisdom as soon as he got me out of the New York City fitness center. We shut it down and walked away. My former partner went on and did her own thing and I'm glad to have inspired her entrepreneurial spirit!

Before getting involved in any kind of business relationship make certain that you have a thorough understanding of not only the other person's credentials and background but also how you will work together as a team. More than half of all business partnerships fail. Some of them fail badly and cost one or both parties a lot of money. So enter into this sort of business marriage as carefully as you would enter into one that involves a wedding ceremony and a diamond ring.

Employee Relations

We really do work like a team at *Body By Jake*, and at Major League Lacrosse too. That's why we are very careful when we hire employees. One bad apple can pretty much spoil the cider, to coin a nifty phrase. I know because I've had a few hires go sour fast. I've seen how one unhappy employee can spread the misery throughout an entire organization.

| *Take care with every hire!*

Sometimes the person is very capable, but his or her personality, skills, or operating methods conflict with the existing culture. It might have been that the people who didn't work out for us were very talented folks who just didn't match up with our casual but hard-charging approach to business. Or, it could be that we have a totally dysfunctional yet highly successful operation that requires a certain insanity to enjoy. I just know that when you hire someone who doesn't fit in, it can be as painful as a root canal until you yank them out. It can also be expensive if you have to give them severance pay and other benefits to make it a clean separation.

If you are going to grow your business, your street-smart success will depend to a great degree on your hiring choices as you grow. You will have to decide when it is time to bring in your first employees, and then when to add more people. My advice, especially to start-up and smaller businesses, is to take equal care in the hiring of each and every employee—from your top managers to the person who opens the mail and empties the waste basket—because you'll be doing that in the beginning anyway. You are the boss, so you have to rely on your instincts about people too.

What Does It Take?

Hiring the right person for the job requires that *you* know exactly what sort of person the job requires. That's easier said (and written) than done, my friends. Take it from ol' Jake. It's especially tough in the sort of start-up operations that I've been involved in. In the early days of Major League Lacrosse, we had a heck of a time finding an executive director. By our fourth season, we'd had three of them. It's not that the people we hired weren't very capable individuals and good folks. The problem was me. You may be shocked to hear this, but the boss can be the source of a problem. You need to acknowledge that and recognize that often when there is a problem with someone you hire, the root cause may be that the job wasn't properly defined or explained to the "problem" person in the first place.

In the early days of the MLL, we really didn't have a good handle on what sort of person we needed in the executive director job. I knew that I didn't want to be the hands-on, day-to-day guy. I've just got too many other irons in the fire with my other businesses. I'm a salesman and motivator at heart, and the old cliché that it's easy to sell a salesman played out in this situation. We hired people who made strong presentations but we didn't give adequate thought to whether they were truly the right individuals for the job. For me, as the founder of a new major league sport, this was an entirely different sort of venture. So, I really was learning on the job too.

Help your employees succeed by steering them straight from the start.

Through trial and error, I realized that we needed a nuts-and-bolts implementer, a person familiar with the lacrosse business. It had to be someone who could deal with the different teams, their owners, managers and players. He had to be able to think on his own, but he also had to be able to take ideas and directions and implement them throughout the league. Eventually, we found someone who had worked as a general manager for one of our teams. That person, David Gross, appears to be working out very well now. We have so much faith in him that we have made him our first league commissioner.

As the boss, your responsibility is to clearly communicate your expectations to your employees. It's up to you to tell the employee that you don't expect to be "protected" from bad news or kept out of the loop if things aren't going exactly as planned. If water pipes are bursting and bad smelly stuff is floating through the warehouse, I want to be told that in very clear and graphic terms so I can get a clear picture of the situation. Keep that in mind when you are thinking about making your first hire and all the hires that follow.

In the early days, you'll have to learn how to pick those people whose skills, knowledge, and experience match the needs of your business. Then, you'll have to figure out how to reward and keep the good people while weeding out those who don't contribute as much as you want them to contribute. You will also have to consider whether you really need to hire people on a full-time basis, or to hire them as needed, or as consultants.

| *If details aren't your thing, hire a micro-manager.*

The most important thing to acknowledge is that every person—and every business person—needs a support team. Back when I was doing fitness training in Hollywood, I didn't have a business team. As my business endeavors grew and expanded into a wide range of enterprises, I had to get street smart about finding people whose strengths either matched up with my weaknesses or who had the skills and knowledge to focus on those things that I didn't have time to pay attention to.

While many businesses are started by trained accountants, lawyers, management experts, and sales and marketing people, very few entrepreneurs are masters of every aspect of business. Sure, most street-smart business people are very familiar with most of their operations—in fact, they'd better be! But there have been a lot of studies to show that most entrepreneurs are better at starting businesses than managing the day-to-day details. That's not always true, but there aren't many people who can do it all. And, it's often the case that people who have the creative drive and energy to see opportunities and transform them into businesses just don't like to get tied down in the day-in and day-out details of actually running a business.

Get Help or Get Out

When my personal fitness training business started to take off in Hollywood, yours truly suddenly needed to be cloned. At first, I tried to maintain an exclusive clientele so I could keep things under control while still making a good living. But everyone in Hollywood is considered an "exclusive client." It's a town where the VIP rooms are bigger than the general admission areas. My phone was ringing off the hook even though I'd never had my number listed. People thought I was playing hard to get, or worse, dodging their calls.

There were certain major stars or power players who tracked me down and offered me such lucrative deals that I just could not refuse them. Yet, I didn't want to shortchange anyone by having too many clients and not enough time to do the job right. Are you getting the picture? Does it sound familiar? I was in a classic stressed-out start-up situation in which the demand exceeded the supply—of me.

Yes, there seemed to be a global shortage of *Body By Jake* at that point in world economic history. I faced the age-old entrepreneurial question: Do I go big or go home? I can laugh about it now, through my tears, because after all these years in businesses I understand that it happens all the time. It's one of the growing pains you'll experience, whether you are starting your own business, buying an existing business, or doing a franchise deal. At some point in every business, you have to decide if it's time to hire more help.

Once again, I'm willing to step up and serve as a *GeeBee*. That's my term for someone who is a "Good Example of a Bad Example." My response to being overstressed in the fitness training field was typical for someone without business training. I hired my two brothers. Hey, they sort of looked like me. They talked like me. And I thought I could train them to do fitness training the way I did fitness training. It seemed like a solution to my problem and a way whereby everybody could go home a winner: me, my clients, and my brothers.

For the sake of peace at future family reunions, let's just say, my efforts to clone myself by hiring my brothers as employees did not work out for all parties. In this case, it was no party at all. I take my share of the blame for that. I may have thought I was ready to be an employer, but I wasn't. Having other people work for you is not as simple as saying "You're hired" and then telling them what to do. Being a boss is tougher than it looks, at least if you want to do it right. And hiring people whose temperaments, skills, knowledge, and experience match up with your own. . .well, that takes a really thoughtful approach.

| *Make sure each hire fits in with the team.*

I would never claim to be a genius at hiring people. But I have learned not to hire anyone until I sit down and do some serious homework about what my business really needs, what I can afford to pay, and where I should look for the right people. The where is worth thinking about. For example, when I was thinking about hiring other people to help my fitness training business, I needed fit folks with people skills. Honesty and discretion were also important since they'd be going to the homes of celebrities and powerful entertainment figures. I couldn't just throw an ad in the newspaper for that job. If I did I might as well have put a headline on it saying, "Well-Built Home Burglars Wanted! Easy Pickin's!"

You've got to put some thought into the kind of people you want to hire for each job. It's not just about credentials like education and experience, it's also about attitude, work ethics, personality traits, style of dress, and other attributes. One of the things I look for in people I hire now is an entrepreneurial attitude. I want them to be so excited about what they do that they are always looking for new opportunities to do what we do better, faster, and more efficiently. A lot of entrepreneurial business owners feel the same way. The founder and CEO of Cobalt Boats, Pack St. Clair, has built his business around employees with entrepreneurial attitudes; as a result his boats have one of the highest customer satisfaction ratings given by the JD Power Awards. By the way, you might be surprised at the type of entrepreneurial employees that this luxury boat maker likes to attract. Are you ready for this?

Farmers!

Cobalt Boats is based in Neodesha, Kansas, population 2,800. There are rivers nearby but the closest lake is two hours away. St. Clair grew up in Neodesha and he kept his entrepreneurial business there because he likes his roots. He also believes in the people there, and they've proven him right. They don't build simple little fishin' boats in Neodesha. Cobalt Boats are sleek. They are priced from the high $30,000s to the even higher $300,000s and up. And they are made by people "with an unstinting, self-reliant work ethic, a can-do farmer's ingenuity, a bred-in-the-bones communal spirit, and perhaps most important of all, an owner's mindset," as St. Clair told *Inc.* magazine. He attributes much of his company's success to the fact that many of his employees come from farm backgrounds.

"Farmers are owners of their own businesses. . . . They understand that things have to get done and get done right or you'll pay for it later," he said in the *Inc.* interview. I'm not suggesting that you have to locate your business or recruit your employees from the sticks. But I do advise you to put as much thought into the character of those you hire as St. Clair does.

Paycheck

Once you've decided to hire someone and thought carefully about what sort of person you want for the job, the next big question for street-smart hiring success is: What do you pay the people you hire? The good news is that there are "Salary Surveys" and "Salary Calculators" all over the World Wide Web these days. You'll find some useful ones at HotJobs.com, Jobstar.org, and salaryexpert.com, which uses Bureau of Labor Statistics data. The accounting firm PricewaterhouseCoopers does an annual "Salary Survey" that offers information across a variety of fields. The Society for Human Resource Management (www.shrm.org) based in Alexandria, Virginia, is also a good source of information about those pesky legal and technical issues that come with growing a business and hiring employees.

Some salary surveys base their information on data submitted by members or users of the Web site, so there is no way to always be sure it is valid information. It's a good idea, then, to check with a couple of sources. The salary or hourly wage you pay someone is just one part of a compensation package for most businesses. There are also stock options, benefits packages, 401(k) plans, and assorted perks that can be part of the deal. Before you delve into the deep pit of wages and benefits, you should give serious thought to whether you truly need someone full-time, or whether you could get by with temporary, part-time, or consulting help. Remember, you don't have to offer health insurance and other benefits to workers who are not full-time.

Whether you hire one person part-time, a full-time person, or a whole room full of people, you should build your team carefully and thoughtfully. When you are the boss of your own business, hiring decisions are up to you. And there are usually two basic reasons for making that decision. One, the work has become too much for you to do yourself. Or two, you don't have certain skills that are needed to keep your business running. Street-smart

entrepreneurs are often strong-willed (okay, stubborn and proud) individu-
alists who sometimes have a hard time admitting that they can't do it all, or
that they don't know it all. Get over that. It's a trap, and your business could
easily go down the tubes if you fall into it.

| *Give your business all the talent it needs to grow.*

If pride is your problem, you should take pride in the fact that your
business is growing and doing so well that you need to bring in more people
to keep up with demand. You also need to go back to the reason you started
your business in the first place: You wanted to do something you could enjoy
and build your life around. No one can enjoy running a business that is
struggling to keep up with demand. You're the boss. You should be able to
take weekends and vacations and the occasional day off without worrying
that the entire business is going to crash and burn while you are on the
beach with the family or friends. If you find yourself feeling trapped in your
own business and unable to enjoy it or to take any time away from it, then
you need to get help or get out.

Hiring Help

Until human cloning becomes a reality, it'll always be tough to find the
"perfect" person who has exactly the skills, personality, temperament, appearance, work ethic, and salary needs that match up with the position. Even
if you do find the ideal candidate, there's no assurance that this person is
going to consider your company the perfect place to work. That brings up
another point. You've got to sell your business to potential employees the
same way you pitched it to your potential investors. Be enthusiastic, but also
be truthful and thorough in describing the hours, work load, pay level, benefits, and outlook for advancement and wage increases. The job candidate
won't stick around long if you present a false picture of your business or the
role he or she will fill. And describing the picnic table in your parking lot as
"our open-air company dining experience" probably isn't a good idea.

| *Get your new hires fired up from Day One!*

Here are more hiring hints to consider for that first hire:

Street-Smart Hiring Hints

▪ Decide exactly what need your business has to fill. Not what you wish you had— like an office masseuse or a gourmet chef—but what your business needs to survive.

▪ Identify the job's exact duties, responsibilities, level of authority, range of pay and benefits, and potential for expanded duties or promotion. Include the level of experience you expect candidates to have, whether this is an entry-, mid-, senior-, or ancient wizard-level position. Also specify what sort of degree is required, from an MBA to a degree in information technology, nursing, communications, cosmetology, automotive engineering, hospitality, or mixology (bartender school).

▪ Compose a *Help Wanted* ad for the job that conveys your enthusiasm and excitement for your business. Don't be afraid to get creative. You don't even have to call it a *Help Wanted* ad, you could call it a "Fun Shared!" ad, which might be more appealing than calling it a "Work Slave Wanted!" advertisement. Show it to your friends and advisors to make sure that it captures the spirit of your company.

▪ Place your ad in the local newspaper and post it on Internet job sites like HotJobs.com as well as in trade publications, or newsletters and magazines from your professional organizations.

▪ Hire or bribe someone else to do the candidate screening so you don't get depressed or panicky. You'll get a lot of calls or e-mails from people who obviously don't fill the bill. That's normal. But it might be helpful for your sanity, to have someone else filter out the people who aren't serious candidates.

▪ Limit the number of people you interview for the job, and don't try to cram too many into one day. It's hard to be charming for hours on end, even for me, Jake Charming!

■ Once you've asked applicants to come to an interview, you owe each of them your full attention without interruptions. Give your complete attention to each applicant—no interruptions or phone calls. Limit your questions to those that pertain to the job. Legally, you can't ask a person's age or marital status. Religion, sex, and politics are off limits too.

■ To give each applicant a fair shot, make sure you read each application and note their qualifications and past experience so you don't waste time making them repeat information you've already got in hand.

■ Remember, you are the boss. You aren't looking for a new best friend. You are hiring an employee. There's nothing wrong with being cordial and warm but if you are going to hire someone you want them to understand from the start that you are in charge and that you will provide them with directions that they will be expected to follow. On the other hand, you should let the potential employee know if you welcome creativity, initiative, and entrepreneurship within your business.

■ Set standards up front for how you expect your employees to dress and behave on the job. As I've said, we have an unusual atmosphere in our *Body By Jake* office. Since our customers don't often visit the office, people pretty much do their own thing. I wear a Polo shirt, jeans, and or tennis shoes on most days but we have some employees who wear ties, and others who prefer T-shirts. As long as people do their jobs well, they pretty much dress as they want, within the limits of good taste, of course.

■ Control the impulse to hire someone on the spot. Even if it is a Harvard grad and trust-fund heir who just wants to work for minimum wage because she or he loves the concept of your business, stifle that urge to say "You're hired." Ask for the names and addresses of former employers and check them out. By the way, I'm not big on other "references" because you never know whether you are talking to someone's favorite uncle or cousin or college roommate. Granted, former employers will often be careful about what they say, but you can read between the lines if you listen carefully.

■ Finally, give yourself time to do a "gut check." I've got to tell you, I rely on that as much or more than anything else when hiring people. I ask myself,

"Is this somebody I want to see and interact with every day in the office?" If I have any sort of bad vibe, I keep looking. You've got to go with that gut feeling when all is said and done. Once you've done that, make your decision and stick with it.

Helping Your New Hires

Your duties as the boss have just begun once you've hired someone. You can't expect a new person to just walk in the first day and feel comfortable. It's your job to help the person get acclimated not only on the first day but over the course of the next several months. The first few days are very important because they can establish how your new hires feel about your business for a long time to come. So be there for them. Spend some time helping them get situated. Show them where to get the supplies they'll need, where the restrooms are located, the lunchroom, the office refrigerator, and the best place for a quick cup of java. If you have other employees, introduce the new person to them.

Even many small businesses often have someone designated to provide formal or informal orientation for the new person, but as the boss, you should make the effort to welcome them and to give them a good feel for where they fit into the organization and its future.

Wise Guys

In all of my businesses, I take final responsibility for the operation, the products and the decisions. But that doesn't mean I don't rely upon and listen to other people. I fill my head with as much information as possible, and that includes asking for advice and listening to the wisdom of people I respect. I learned to do that early on when I was a newcomer to Hollywood and the entertainment industry, and I've worked hard at maintaining that attitude even after achieving a certain level of street-smart success. I've seen a lot of other very successful people lose touch and take hard falls because they felt they no longer needed anybody else. I don't want to make that mistake and I don't want you to make it either.

| *Count on a numbers cruncher!*

I've been really fortunate to have a big circle of willing and wise advisors who've helped me over the years. In my case, these are mostly members of my informal "cabinet," but you might want to make it a more formal arrangement by putting together an advisory board or even a more structured board of directors, who are paid—in shares or salaries or both—to monitor your business operations. Depending on your type of business and its needs, you can hire role players as full-time employers, on retainer, as consultants, or as members of a board of directors or advisory board.

The two most critical role players you will need on your team are a legal eagle and a numbers cruncher. In the early days of your business, you probably can get by with simply hiring an attorney or an accountant as you need their services. As your business grows, you may need to put an attorney and an accountant on retainer, or even hire them as in-house employees. Without a doubt, you will need an attorney to advise you on legal matters and to protect you from lawsuits at all stages of your operation. Few small businesses can afford an "in house" counsel, but most will need to have an attorney familiar with their operations.

Whether you keep one on retainer or simply pay as you go, I'd encourage you to build a relationship with an attorney you trust and genuinely enjoy being with. I've had a long relationship with mine, Robert Lieberman, and he has watched my back faithfully over the years. Early on in my business, I made the mistake of hiring a "manager," who nearly managed me right out of business. After that, I managed myself and relied on my trusted attorney to look out for me. I pay him for his services when I need them, but his friendship and guidance are equally important.

Just recently, we hired a full-time chief financial officer. We made that move after taking the big step up from serving primarily as a product licensing company to developing and marketing our own products. That was a very big decision that altered our whole approach to business. So we had to bring in a serious money guy, or as we call him, "our designated grown-up." Just a few years ago, we wouldn't have been in a position to bring in someone of Kevin Gallagher's caliber. He wears a dress shirt and tie, for crying out loud.

Kevin joined us after working as a trouble-shooting chief executive and chief financial officer at several major and international corporations. He has a master's degree in finance and an undergraduate degree in business administration. And since he has joined our company, he's helped move us into position to be a much bigger player in the health and fitness industry. At this stage in our growth it is vital to have a guy like Kevin on board. He brings us greater credibility with financial institutions because he can talk the lingo with bankers and investors, and with companies that we might want to buy or companies that might want to invest in us. I have my rap-a-doo and Phil can talk widgets and whirligigs in depth, but neither of us has the sort of financial background that Kevin brings to the big-people table.

If you put together a board of directors or an advisory board for your start-up, I'd recommend having a legal eagle and a numbers cruncher on board, as well as a marketing sales "gee whiz" person with a lot of enthusiasm. Look for retired executives from your field who might be interested in serving as advisors or board members. Their experience and contacts can protect you from making mistakes and help you grow your business. It can also be really helpful to join groups like the Chamber of Commerce, the Jaycees, the Young Entrepreneurs Organization, or the Young Presidents Club, where you are likely to find people willing to serve as mentors, role models, or advisors.

Get a Go-To

Aside from your employees, management team, and board members, it is sometimes helpful also to have smart and creative friends you can go to when you need to bounce an idea off someone, or get an unfiltered reality check. I call these my "Go-To" People. If you are lucky, you have a few folks like this in your personal life and in your professional life. For kids, it's often a favorite aunt, uncle, neighbor, or grandparent. In the movie *Cast Away,* Tom Hanks' Go-To Person was a volleyball he called Wilson. I'm sure they bounced a lot of ideas off each other on that lonely island, but my sense is that sporting goods should not be your primary source for solace, encouragement, advice, and support.

When I was growing up, I had a "Go-To" Grams, my grandmother, Myra Duberstein. She took it upon herself to show me as much of the world as she could. Strangely enough, my Grams was pretty well connected. She managed the Manhattan Beach Hotel back in the day when a lot of celebrities passed through its doors. She was like the housemother for regular guests and for all the parties and family gatherings. Grams was there when both Neil Sedaka and Neil Diamond were bar mitzvahed, if you can believe that. She always brought me along when something special was going on. My grandmother wanted me to see more of the world than Brooklyn. Because of her hotel contacts, she could get tickets to Yankee games and Forest Hills tennis matches. She took me to Aqueduct and Belmont racetracks. She was a great lady who really opened my eyes to a lot of life.

In fact, it was my Go-To Grams who took me to see *Hair*, the wild and wooly rock musical on Broadway, when I was in fifth grade. We sat in the first row where I really did see a famous person naked, though I didn't know it at the time. I discovered it years later, when I was training my first client, the actress Sandy Will. She was then the girlfriend, and later the wife, of actor Keith Carradine. I started training Keith too, and one day he told me that he'd been in the cast of *Hair*. We figured out that he was one of the stars in the show when I saw it with Grams.

"Jake, I can't believe it, you've seen me naked," he said.

I hated to burst his bubble, but I never noticed him. I was looking at the girls!

From *Hair* to the Yankees, I saw it all thanks to my Grams. She was there for me as a kid. She wanted me to see and experience all sorts of things, and she was always extremely supportive of everything I did. Just like your Go-To Person should be for you.

| *Get Your Go-To People!*

There is a tendency in entrepreneurial businesses to think you've got to be totally focused on the success of your company, but in truth, the most successful street-smart entrepreneurs are those who pay as much attention to their business relationships as their personal relationships. (Cue the Streisand: "People, people who need people . . .")

Seriously now, it's true. Nobody builds a successful business alone. So don't isolate yourself. Build a network of Go-To People you can talk to and lean on.

Last December we had two companies interested in buying into *Body By Jake*. We were flattered and excited about that but over the holidays I started wondering if this was something I really wanted to do. Once you sell a piece of your company it will usually cost you a lot more to buy it back. I had talked to my friend Pete Musser, who was the CEO and founder of Safeguard Scientific. I reached out to Pete and he counseled me by saying that he didn't see why I would do it. "You shouldn't be selling, you should be buying," he said. He told me to look at buying companies that would help me expand my business instead. He said, "Jake, be in control of your destiny!" His outside perspective really helped me understand my own business and its place in the market.

| *Make it a two-way street!*

I only hope I can return the favor some day. That is an important point, by the way. This is a two-way street. You can't expect other people to be there for you all the time unless you are willing to step up for them. I have served as the Go-To Person for a whole bunch of friends. Also, you should understand that it takes time to develop a network of Go-To People. The relationship has to be built on mutual trust. If people sense that your only motivation for establishing a relationship is pure self-interest, you will never be able to build trust. You have to be willing to lend a hand if you expect others to do it for you. When you earn a reputation for being a stand up Go-To Person, you'll be amazed to see the connections you can make—and the people you will attract to join you in street-smart business success.

To find street-smart success, you've got to buy into the belief that there is enough success out there for everybody. You are going to run into people who don't think that way. They have a *scarcity mentality*. They think there is only so much success out there, like a pie with a limited number of slices. That's a miser's way of thinking, and it's a miserable way to live.

I believe in an abundance mentality. I think there's a whole universe out there with unlimited opportunities for street-smart success. I've grabbed a lot of it and I'll be tickled silly when you can reach up and grab some too. There's enough for everyone. Your piece of the pie is waiting. Don't let anyone tell you there's not enough. Jake says there's more than enough!

digging for dough

THERE'S NOTHING as exciting as starting a business built around something you love to do. Unfortunately, getting a new business up and running almost always requires doing something that most people really hate to do—borrowing money. Yet, it's one of those things that you've got to do, which is yet another reason that you have to really be pumped up about your business, whatever it may be.

Believe me, you will hear a lot of "no's" in your search for a "yes" when it comes to digging for the dough.

The first person I ever went to for a business loan was one of my best buddies and clients, Steven Spielberg. It wasn't like I just tracked down the richest guy I knew and asked him for money. Wiels and I had a real bond. I thought of him as a brother. Still, even asking a brother for a loan is not an easy thing to do. I was nervous about it. We'd done a lot of hanging out together. He'd taken me to his movie locations around the world to train Harrison Ford and other actors, but also to just be there as a friend who didn't expect any favors. (Rumor had it that I was his first choice for the Indiana Jones role. He just decided to go with a less muscular actor instead!)

I trust in his wisdom. We've always trusted each other. We'd talked for hours about our plans and dreams as we traveled or during our workouts. Wiels has the heart of a street-smart entrepreneur. He encouraged me to develop the *Body By Jake* brand into a real business. When my partner Phil Scotti and I started looking at doing a chain of fitness centers in luxury hotels and resorts around the country in 1990, I thought Wiels might want to get involved in the opportunity. I really thought it was an investment that would pay off for him or I wouldn't have asked.

I went to his beach house on a Saturday morning and I laid it out for him as something that we could do together that would profit both of us. I saw in his face right away that he didn't feel comfortable with the idea.

"Jake, I know you'll be super-successful with this. But the fact is that if I didn't like you so much, I'd probably do this in a heartbeat. It's just that I don't ever want to risk our friendship in a business deal," he said.

He must have thought that I looked disappointed, but really I was just sorry that I'd put strain on the friendship by asking.

"You can take this as me blowing you off, or as what it really is: a friend not wanting to risk the friendship," he said.

I saw his point and I accepted him at his word. It turned out for the best. I eventually found the financing I needed and Wiels and I are still good buddies. Yet, I was disappointed at the time, and to this day I regret that I asked him. I can't argue with his wanting to keep our friendship clean of money ties. It's always a tough call whether or not to go to friends and family for startup money. You never know for certain how people will react. If you are close to someone who has the ability to provide financing, it's very tempting to reach out to them. Many business startups are financed that way. But in some ways, I think Wiels did me a favor. If he'd anted up, it would have been, in a sense, the easy way out, and I wouldn't have learned as much about the challenges of financing a business.

Finding the funds to get a business started and to keep it going is probably the biggest stumbling block that street-smart entrepreneurs encounter, especially with their first businesses. I'm afraid Mark Twain was right when he said, "Banks will lend you money if you can prove you don't need it." Once you've had some success creating cash flow with a business, banks and other lenders will come knocking on your door.

> *Be prepared to scrape and beg for bucks in the early days. It'll keep you humble when you are raking in the dough later!*

It might help a little, maybe just a very little, to know that every one who has ever owned a business has gone through the same thing at some point. Finding funds is like a rite of passage for street-smart entrepreneurs. It'll help to know what your options are and to understand going in what the upsides and downsides of each option are.

Here are five unconventional ways to raise money for your business:

1. Win the lottery

2. Discover sunken treasure

3. Auction your vital organs on eBay

4. Sign yourself up for indentured servitude

5. Convince Donald Trump that you are his love child

Well, I told you they were unconventional methods. Now let's look at some far more conventional sources of start-up financing:

1. Your money

2. A friend's money

3. Family money

4. A bank's money

5, A bunch of people's money (venture capitalists)

Self-Financing

You've got to admit, the unconventional ideas were more fun, but the conventional sources are far more practical. Studies say that most new businesses are financed by the owner's personal savings, selling stocks and bonds, taking out second mortgages or home equity loans, and, scary as it may be, maxing out credit cards. I gotta tell you, I did take out a second mortgage on my house once to help the business, but that's a risk I took after some careful thought. Robert Townsend, a friend of mine, once financed a movie with his credit cards, but it's still a very dicey way to go. I didn't own a credit card until I was twenty-five. So, let it be known right here and now that your street-smart success advisor does not advocate that you finance your first business by running your credit cards up to the limit. That is not a street-smart way to success. It's more like a really dumb way to end up deep in debt.

It's perfectly fine to use credit cards to make purchases when your business is profitable and you've got good cash flow. But it's suicidal to rack up credit-card debt when your business has yet to get on its feet. You can't run a business while you are standing in a financial hole. Credit-card interest rates will eat up what little profits most start-ups can generate in the first six months, and they always want more. That's real money you are playing with, and if you don't pay off credit-card debt your credit ratings will drop, which will make it impossible to rent property, lease equipment, and get loans in the future.

So, don't go that route unless you are certain that you'll be able to get *all* of your credit-card balances paid off before you get buried. In fact, even though personal savings are the most common source of funding for new businesses, I really discourage you from doing anything that might consume all of your personal funds, especially if you have a family to support. It's one thing to be young and single and take financial risks. It's an entirely different matter to put your family's welfare on the line. I hate the sight of children crying on the curb with their toys piled in boxes, don't you?

Before you get tempted to take out a second mortgage or cash out the 401(k) and eat all those tax penalties, think about what could go wrong if your business goes sour. If you've got plenty of cash reserves, go for it. But don't risk losing your family's home or financial security without giving very serious thoughts to the consequences. There are many other alternatives to consider before doing that. We're going to take a look at the many options available but *first*, you need to get a good handle on exactly how much money you'll need to open the door to your new business and keep it running for at least those challenging first six months or so.

If you bet the farm on your new business, be prepared to sleep with the chickens.

WHAT'S IT GOING TO TAKE TO OPEN THE DOORS?

There's no one-size-fits-all approach to determining exactly how much it will take to get your start-up started up. Ten million dollars is a nice round figure, and that would probably get most bike repair shops and lawn services rolling, but if you are going to ask other people for money, you've got to keep it real. Your street-smart success is going to depend on coming up with a solid financial plan that includes enough money to meet the specific needs of your business at start-up and every stage beyond.

If you're going to work out of your garage and you've already got all the office equipment you need, that's great. You can probably get by without having to tap the global financial reserves for more than a couple bucks. But you'd better make sure that you haven't missed something crucial to the operation of your business. You don't want to have a full-page ad in the paper announcing your grand opening and then discover that, oops, you forgot about cash registers or computer servers. It's always embarrassing when you have to usher those first customers back out the door and ask them to come back later.

Let's look at your business and figure out what it's going to take to get rocking.

1. *Start-Up Expenses.* You're going to need things that won't be recurring expenses but still are initial hits to the budgets. These can include legal fees and processing costs of forming a limited liability corporation (L.L.C.) or a regular corporation. You might have big cash outlays if you are buying a building or some big piece of equipment. Then there are those other expenses that just eat away at your reserves, like getting telephone service and other utilities hooked up; creating a Web site; signs; office equipment; city, state, and federal licenses; and the coffee maker and refrigerator for the break room. The pool table may have to wait.

2. *Continuing Expenses.* Next, you have to look at continuing expenses, which include both *fixed expenses* like rent and *varied expenses* for things like

the utility bills and employee salaries. Your fixed expenses and overhead costs should include mortgage payments or rent for the office, and insurance payments. Your variable expenses and production costs include electricity, water, and phone bills; office supplies; salaries and benefits; Internet service; postal or express mail service; inventory costs; shipping and packaging costs; sales commissions; and all other costs that come with selling your products or providing your service.

To put it all together, create a worksheet listing the essentials in both start-up and continuing expense categories. Here is a list of items that should go on your worksheet:

One-Time Start-Up Costs

1. Down payment and security deposits on property, decorating, and remodeling

2. Fixtures and equipment

3. Installation of fixtures and equipment

4. Initial inventory

5. Utility deposits and hookup

6. Legal, accounting, and other professional fees

7. Local, state, and federal licenses and permits

8. Advertising and promotion for opening

9. Consulting and software

10. Cash

11. Other

Monthly (Continuing) Expenses

1. Your salary (if any)

2. All other salaries, wages, and benefits

3. Rent or mortgage payment

4. Advertising

5. Delivery expenses

6. Supplies

7. Telephone

8. Utilities

9. Insurance

10. Taxes, including Social Security

11. Interest on loans

12. Maintenance

13. Legal and other professional fees

14. Miscellaneous

Calculate your total start-up costs. You can do this on a worksheet, or you can look on the Internet for start-up cost calculators. Two that are recommended by the U.S. Small Business Administration are:

1. Palo Alto Startup Cost Estimator
   (www.bplans.com/contentkit/index.cfm?s = tools&affiliate = sba)

2. Business Know-How Startup Calculator
   (www.businessknowhow.net/bkh/startup.htm)

Funds from Friends

The second most common source of funding for start-ups is friends and family. My experiences asking friends to invest has been both good and not so good. I met famed television director and producer Aaron Spelling while training his wife Candy at their home, and he really liked the idea of getting involved in my business projects. Aaron, the son of a Sears tailor, is the creator of some of the longest running television series, including *Beverly Hills 90210* (costarring his daughter Tori) as well as *Charlie's Angels, Dynasty,* and *The Love Boat*. He lives in one of the biggest mansions in Hollywood, but he's also a guy known for his generosity. Once Wiels decided he didn't want to be an investor, I decided to go to Aaron with my idea to put *Body By Jake* fitness studios in resort hotels. Although it's scary to think about now, at the time I offered Aaron a 50-percent stake in the business for $500,000. He jumped on the idea and told me to work it out with his accountant. But his numbers cruncher crunched our deal. "Jake, my accountant said that economic conditions aren't right for this deal and he won't let me do it," Aaron told me.

Now, I know that Aaron could have overruled his accountant, but rich people don't get rich by tuning out their financial advisors. Aaron was straight with me and I wasn't going to try to argue finances with his expert. In truth, his accountant was right. Phil and I had gotten excited because we'd scored a huge success in 1990 by landing the first franchise deal for a *Body By Jake* Health Studio at a Disney property—the Dolphin Hotel in Orlando. But a recession hit just as we were rolling out our concept for other big resort hotels. Nearly all of them loved the idea, but most said our timing was lousy. Even the best resorts were having trouble filling their rooms so their focus was on putting heads in beds, not pumping up the patrons. We eventually pulled back and looked for other opportunities.

I shudder to think about it now because if Aaron had come in as a full partner for $500,000, his shares in *Body By Jake* today would be worth many times his original stake. I'd be kicking myself for selling it so cheap. Remember that when you are seeking financing for your company. Don't give away the store. If you believe in your concept and if there is any other way to raise money, don't give away your ownership. Hang on to as much of your own company as you can. Today, I'm very glad that I didn't sell off half the company, and I'm sure Aaron doesn't stay up nights crying about it either. He's still able to pay the light bills at his mansion.

| *Is banking on friends in your best interest?*

Financing deals with friends can work out fine for everyone under the right circumstances. Later in the book, I'll tell you about some far more successful partnerships I've had with friends like Tim Robertson of The Family Channel, who has been an investor in several of my enterprises, including FitTV and Major League Lacrosse. Tim and I have had amazing success in our partnerships. But it is also true that we first became friends after we started doing business together. I'm more cautious now about asking my personal friends to invest in my businesses, and it's something you should be very careful about doing too. For one thing, even if your business dealings are going very well, it's hard to "just be friends" and enjoy each other's company when you've got shared business interests. No matter how hard you try, you can't escape or avoid talking about business when you get together, and that makes it hard to just relax with your buddies. So keep that in mind. Unless you've got a friend with deep, deep pockets who can easily take the loss if things go sour, you should consider whether getting the financial help now is worth losing a friend later.

The Family Plan

Asking family members for financial help in starting a business is such a traditional and natural financing method that people often get into it without really thinking it through carefully. I'd advise you to give it a lot of thought. Sometimes those closest to you may not make the best business partners, but it is also true that family businesses are one of the greatest assets of our nation.

Nearly 60 percent of the publicly held companies in the United States are family controlled. Ford Motors, Wal-Mart, and Anheuser-Busch are just a few of the great companies that are controlled by families. In fact, nearly 35 percent of family-controlled businesses are Fortune 500 companies. Family-owned businesses account for 60 percent of employment, half of the gross domestic product, and 65 percent of all wages paid in the United States, according to the Cox Family Enterprise Center at Kennesaw State University in Georgia.

Family firms also account for 80 percent of the world's businesses. It's an American tradition, but it's practiced also in many nations as well as by all types of Americans. Korean, Chinese, and Asian Indians have their own networks of friends and families, who've helped them establish dominance in businesses like dry cleaners, convenience stores, and motels in many parts of the country.

It's tempting to go to family members for start-up funds because they'll often give you the money interest free or at a much lower rate than a bank or venture capital investor. That's great if it works out for everyone. But make sure you get all of the specifics down on paper and agreed to by all parties so that there are no misunderstandings that lead to a food fight at the Fourth of July picnic. Don't borrow money from family members who can't afford to lose the investment. Don't promise that they'll get rich in the deal. And if you care about your family relationships, pay them back before you buy the country-club membership, the house in Hawaii, or the Ferrari.

| *The best family to tap for funds is the Rockefellers.*

Another thing to consider when asking family members to help finance your start-up is whether or not you are asking them simply to invest their money, or are you asking them to be part of your day-to-day business too? Without a doubt there are many successful businesses in which family members work together, but again, this is something that you need to think about very carefully. The survival rate for family-owned firms is not great overall. Only 30 percent are passed on to the second generation, and only 10 percent make it to the third.

Running any business is a challenge, but a family business adds a whole new dynamic to the usual issues of dealing with cash flow, competition, market demand, and employees. It can also really mess up Thanksgiving dinner and Christmas Eve. Before you tap family funds, keep in mind that there will likely be no escaping business talk at the dinner table, or family talk in the office. That's not necessarily a bad thing, but it is something you need to understand going in. I've heard horror stories of younger brothers who borrowed money from older brothers to start businesses and then were late or slow to repay the loans. This triggered mini-wars between the sisters-in-law and other family members that went on for years. Don't let that happen to you.

To deal with that family dynamic, it's best to set up formal processes to foster communication and to maintain a professional operation. If you ask family members to invest in the business, make certain that you have written agreements that detail exactly what their roles will be in the business. Will they work there too? Will they serve on a board of advisors? If you are trading shares in the company for investment capital, create a formal process and established times for shareholders to meet and offer their input on the business. Then, you might want to establish a family council or family advisory board to deal with family issues related to the business.

Remember that older brother who used to pin you to the ground and call you "Wimpy?" You don't want him doing that in front of your employees do you? What if your mother barged into an important meeting with a client and demanded that you clean up the supply room before you do another thing? Well, those scenarios may seem far-fetched, but anyone who has ever been involved in a family business can tell you that family issues can become problems unless you take measures to keep things on a business level.

You don't want family members—or any shareholders—looking over your shoulder every day and second-guessing how you run the business. But if they invest in the business, they should be able to offer suggestions and contribute to your planning for it. Structure is important in any enterprise but especially in a family business, because family members may fall back on family hierarchies in the absence of other, formal organization. Mission statements and corporate governance rules are a good idea because they keep everyone focused on the business.

It's probably a good idea also to create written guidelines on when the next generation should start becoming involved both as employees and as shareholders. It can be helpful to have five-, ten- and even fifteen-year plans in place so that there is a formal structure. Experts often recommend that young and ambitious family members work elsewhere for at least a few years to gain perspective and to get fresh ideas that might help the family operation down the line. And, while we're on this topic, family businesses need to do very careful estate planning with professionals who can help avoid the pitfalls that many family-owned businesses fall into.

Most sports team owners are well aware of what happened in the case of Miami's Robbie family. The patriarch, Joe Robbie, built a sports empire around his Miami Dolphins NFL team. He even owned the stadium where they played. But after his death in 1990, followed by the death of his wife, their children had to sell off everything to pay estate taxes, estimated at nearly $47 million, according to a *Miami Herald* report. In any business, it's important to plan ahead and make sure your family and your employees are taken care of if something happens to you.

Going to the Bank

Being street smart about business means knowing how to play the game. And when it comes to borrowing money from a bank, you've got to play by the bank's rules. You don't just walk in and ask them to hand you a blank check. You've got to know exactly what it will take to open the doors of your business and to keep it running until the cash starts flowing.

My friends, once again, this is why you really have to be pumped up about your business. You've also got to know it upside down and inside out so that the bankers will see that you've got your heart and soul invested in your dream. Believe it or not, banks make money by lending it. They want to lend money to people, but only to people who meet their standards when it comes to their ability to pay back the money—plus interest. Still, it's funny that for every story you hear about some poor struggling start-up that can't get a loan to save its soul, you hear five stories about bank executives who've loaned millions of dollars to con artists whose only assets were the ability to tell big lies with straight faces.

Accept it. The world isn't fair, especially when it comes to asking banks for loans. Now that we've acknowledged that, get over it. Yes, it's true, bankers are the kind of people who will lend you an umbrella when the sun is shining and then demand that you give it back as soon as the first raindrops hit the sidewalk. Deal with it. If you need cash to open the doors of your business, you're going to have to learn to play nice with the money guys. And you've got to know how to speak their lingo. Of course, it also helps to know what to ask for once you sit down with the loan officer. There are two types of basic business loans: One, those that cost an arm and a leg. And two, those that cost an arm, a leg, and your first-born child.

But seriously, the two basic types of business loans would be:

1. *Short-Term*: For your purposes these range from a few months to a year and are useful for working capital, accounts receivable, and lines of credit.

2. *Long-Term*: These are mostly used for big money real estate and equipment purchases and other expenses like construction, furniture, trucks, and other work vehicles.

Okay, so now you know what the bank has to offer you, let's look at what you have to offer the bank. There are two major things to keep in mind when you walk into your neighborhood U.S. bank:

1. You've got to be able to repay to play.

2. Clean credit counts.

1. YOU'VE GOT TO BE ABLE TO REPAY TO PLAY

Your friendly banker wants to keep her job and move up the bank ladder, so when she does a loan application interview with you, she doesn't care that you went to high school with her second cousin's girlfriend. Nor does she care that you were an all-conference volleyball setter, or that you spent $1,500 on your "meet the bankers" suit. She wants to know what sort of risk you represent.

It's all about the risk:

One early Bad Risk warning sign: Someone who asks for a loan without knowing exactly how much he needs.

Another early Bad Risk warning sign: Someone who is not prepared to show how she'll pay back that loan.

To get a loan, you've got to have a clue. You've got to be prepared and organized, and that's where your business plan comes in real handy. It forces you to think through every stage of your business, and to put it all down on paper. So when you go to get your first business loan from a bank, your business plan will be your best tool for prying the money out of their vaults. If you've done your homework, you should know exactly how much money you need, why you need it, and how you will pay it back.

But you'll still have to convince the bankers that you are worth the risk, which means they'll want to know if you are good for the dough. When a bank loan officer puts together your loan package, she has to provide evidence that you have the ability to repay the loan based on the terms everyone has agreed to, whether it's a six-month loan, a five-year loan, or a ten-year loan. The bank's loan approval police will want to see at least two sources of income that can be used to pay back the loan.

Since you are approaching them as a street-smart entrepreneur with a new business, they'll want to see proof that your start-up will have some cash flow. They'll also want to know what sort of personal savings, property, stocks, and bonds you've got stashed away. If you are buying an existing business, the prospective lender will want to take a look at its cash flow and past financial records. If your business is a start-up, they'll want to see solid evidence that you'll be able to repay the loan on time in the business plan.

Your banker will ask what "equity" you have in the business, which means what value the business has over and above whatever money you've put into it. Hopefully, the value of your business will increase, creating equity for you as you build it up, just as, in most cases, the value of your home increases because of market demand and improvements you make. It's pretty standard that banks and other financial institutions will only loan money to an existing business if the total liabilities (or debt) of a business are no more than four times the amount of equity. So, if you want Mr. Banker to give you a loan, you've got to make sure you have enough equity in the business to swing the loan.

Sometimes, even street-smart rookies are shocked to discover that banks won't just hand over all of the money they need to start a business. If only it was that easy. Unless you find the most generous banker in the U.S. of A., you will be expected to ante up some of your own green. The amount that you've got to slap down depends on the type of loan you're getting, its purpose, and the terms of the loan agreement. As a general rule, your bank will want you to put down between 20 and 40 percent. So if you say you'll need $100,000 to get your pet grooming salon going, figure that the bank will want you to put up $20,000 to $40,000, and it will kick in the rest.

| Money talks. So learn the lingo.

Your banker might talk about the "debt to equity" ratio, which compares the total amount *owed* to the total amount *owned*. The formula is total liabilities divided by total equity (or total stockholder equity) multiplied by 100 to give a percentage. So, if your banker made you ante up $20,000 before kicking in the $80,000 loan to give you the $100,000 you need, the debt to equity ratio would be 4:1.

I don't know about you, but all this bank stuff is making my brain numb. I just want you to be familiar with the terms so you don't start twitching when the banker throws it out. *Collateral* is another term you'll hear. Basically, collateral is anything you own that can be sold or cashed in to pay back the loan in case your business goes belly-up. If all you own is a couple bar stools and a waterbed, you'll probably have to get someone with deeper pockets to co-sign on your business loan.

Even if you own a nice condominium with brand new furniture, you shouldn't figure that the bank will put the same value on them as your real estate agent or the local used furniture dealer. Banks also take into account what it will cost to "liquidate" (scary word) your assets, which means things like realtor fees, taxes, and depreciation will be subtracted from the value of your collateral.

2. CLEAN CREDIT COUNTS

Remember the parking tickets you ignored? The final rent check that you skipped out on? The past due balance on your credit card? This is where those "little" black marks on your financial record can come back to haunt you. You can bet that one of the very first things most financial institutions will do when reviewing your loan application is to check your personal and business credit. So you may have a little clean up to do in Aisle One before you go money-shopping for your new business.

Your first stop should be the shelf marked Internal Revenue Service. If you haven't been paying or if you are behind in your taxes, you can expect the banker to pull out the hot lights and brass knuckles for some heavy interrogation. A lot of business loans are run through government partnerships and agencies, and they tend to feel that if you haven't been paying your taxes then you shouldn't benefit from their programs. So get right with Uncle Sam before you go to the bank.

| *Protect your good credit from the bad guys.*

Even if you've never skipped a tax payment or fallen behind on the rent, it's a good idea to check your credit history just to make certain there are no black marks on your record. Mistakes are common in credit histories, and so is out-and-out fraud. Identity theft has become increasingly common, and other people can mess up your credit history without your knowledge. To make certain that you don't have credit problems before you go looking for start-up money, start your credit check at least three months before you contact a lender. You can get your own personal credit report by contacting one of the three major credit bureaus:

Equifax: 800-685-1111; P.O. Box 740241, Atlanta, GA 30374; www.equifax.com

Experian: 888-397-3742 ; P.O. Box 2002, Allen, TX 75013; www.experian.com.

TransUnion: 800-888-4213; P.O. Box 2000, Chester, PA 19022; www.transunion.com.

Yes, they have your file. I don't know about Santa Claus, but Big Brother knows if you've been bad or good. Don't be shocked if you find inaccuracies and out-of-date material in your credit reports. It happens all the time and it is usually easy enough to clear up. In many cases, people find old medical bills that have been paid by insurers but are still listed as unpaid by hospitals, or items that were bought on credit and paid off but are still reported as unpaid on your credit history. The first thing you should look for are mistakes in your name, social security number, and address. Mistakes in that basic information can result in you being tagged with someone else's credit problems. If that information is correct, check out the rest of the report, which lists your credit history for credit cards, mortgages, student loans, rent-to-own television sets, car leases, and anything else you bought on the payment plan.

In most cases, the loans that weren't paid off or weren't paid on time will be listed first on your credit report. Those bad boys can hurt your ability to get a loan for your business, so get them straightened out pronto! It probably won't hurt if your credit report says you were late a couple times in making payments, but if you have a history of being late often, or if you missed payments altogether, it could scare off a lender. If your bad credit was the result of some hard times, like a divorce or a medical crisis, you should still be able to get a loan if you can show that before the hard times hit you had a good payment history.

If you suspect fraud on your credit report, notify your credit bureau and they will guide you through the process. Remember that it can take a month or more to get mistakes or problems cleared up on your credit history, so that's another reason to check yours out long before you start looking for start-up money at a bank or any other financial institution.

Venturing Beyond Banks

Where do you go for start-up cash if you don't have the money yourself, your family and friends are tapped out, and your neighborhood bank president was your prom date who went home with the quarterback instead of you?

Well, do you believe in *angels*?

In the world of high and low finance, angels don't come with halos and wings. They're more likely to have calculators and risk tables. Sources of private funding can be individual "angels" or venture capital firms that have a large pool of money from groups of investors they represent. Just because they call them angels doesn't mean they are full of grace. Some are definitely full of other things. Private investors can range from rich-kid chuckleheads who are playing with their father's trust fund money to former dot-com executives who got out when the getting was good. Still others are professional investors who are shrewd money-making machines. Some of them truly want to see you succeed. Others have been known to intentionally tie up entrepreneurs in bad deals so they can come in and take over their businesses when they fail.

> *Just because they call them angels doesn't mean they are full of grace.*

Unlike bankers and most financial institutions, angels and venture capital investors will likely want a piece of your company's future profits in exchange for their financial support. If you don't repay on time, they'll want an even bigger piece. These guys don't fool around. You should never give up so much of your company that you lose control of it. Don't ever sign an agreement with them without having a lawyer and/or an expert accountant examine it to protect your interests. And before you sign on the dotted line, always check with other people who've borrowed money from them to see how they felt they were treated.

Venture capitalists can be loan sharks in nicer suits. They usually want a 30 to 35 percent risk-adjusted annual return on their investments. Their goal is to get back six times their investment in three to five years. They are not your pals. They are in the game to make money for themselves. Most of the time, they really could care less about your dreams or your desire to one day own a nice house in Hilton Head or in the Hamptons. That's not to say they are bad people, they are simply people that you should deal with in a very careful and straightforward manner because they don't mess around. If you need their help, they will give it, but the price is likely to be high if your business succeeds and even higher if it doesn't.

I have gone out a couple times to raise money, and it's always come back to me deciding to invest my own money in the company instead. The angels or venture capitalists may be great guys, but in the end, they are going to want a say in your business. If that works for you, go ahead and do it, but know that they will want a chair at the table in your office conference room. You don't get something for nothing. Giving up equity is one thing, but you have to be ready to give up part of the control of your business. In most cases, entrepreneurs want it done their way.

Venture capitalists will demand to know exactly what they are getting into, so expect them to go over your numbers like a diamond cutter checking out a raw rock. They will also want to have a very specific exit strategy plotted out once their financial involvement in your business is complete. Your plan should include a timetable plus projected returns on their investment. Keep in mind that when some angels and venture capital people make a loan to a business owner, they feel it gives them the right to tell the owner how to run the business. If you're like most street-smart entrepreneurs, you won't like that much. The real pros in private lending will monitor your business very carefully and you can be sure they'll let you know if they think you are screwing up, but they'll usually do it in a way that you'll welcome, or at least in a way you won't resent.

| *Money players don't play around.*

Many top venture capital firms operate quietly, so quietly you may have a hard time finding them. A lot of them specialize in certain markets, like manufacturing, high tech, biotech, or entertainment ventures. You may have to talk to professional organizations or trade groups to find venture capitalists who loan money in your field. Here are a couple of sources to help get you started up in your search for start-up funds:

National Association of Small Business Investment Companies
666 11th Street, NW
Suite 750
Washington, DC 20001
(202) 628-5055

National Venture Capital Association
1655 North Ft. Myer Drive, #850
Arlington, VA 22209
(703) 524-2549

Entrepreneurial Management Center
5250 Campanile Drive
San Diego, CA 92182
(619) 594-2781
Web site: www.sdsu.edu/emc

If your business has a real societal benefit, such as helping the environment or assisting the needy, you might also check out the Investors' Circle, one of the country's oldest and largest investor networks dedicated to nurturing businesses that help society. Its members and active affiliates are high net-worth individuals, professional venture capitalists, family offices, and foundations. They only assist businesses in five specific areas: energy/environment, food/organics, community development, education/media, and

health/wellness. They especially encourage minority and women-led businesses. You can contact them at:

Investors' Circle
320 Washington Street
Brookline, MA 02445
(617) 566-2600
Web site: inbox@investorscircle.net

There are also angels and venture-capital funds linked to federal, state,
and local programs like the Small Business Administration. Many colleges
and universities have small business incubator programs that help link entrepreneurs to sources of funding. Cities and towns also often have community
development grant programs for encouraging business growth. You can learn
about a lot of these programs at the Small Business Administration Investment Division in Washington, D.C. Call them at (202) 205-6510, or check
out their Web site: www.sba.gov/INV/.

TOUCHED BY AN ANGEL

Some financial angels are truly heaven-sent, but some may seem like they
come from much lower, much warmer places. Don't get me wrong, private
investors can be terrific. Like most street-smart entrepreneurs, I ran into a
few scalawags before I finally found the good guys. When I saw the opportunity to create a television network devoted to health and fitness, I took the
idea to Tim Robertson, who is probably the closest thing I've seen to the
ideal "angel" investor. Tim is one of the true good guys. He doesn't invest in
other people's businesses. He invests in their dreams. Believe me, I know.

Back in late 1989, I came up with an idea for a sitcom that I sold to CBS.
I had a lot going on because I'd also renewed my *Body By Jake* show in first-
run syndication with Sam Goldwyn, Jr. But then, just as I was heading out
the door to Houston to promote the fitness show at the annual convention
for the National Association of Television Program Executives (NATPE), I
got word that my CBS deal had fallen through because of changes in top
management there.

I was disappointed but I put it out of my mind temporarily so I could focus on promoting my fitness show at the convention. I was signing T-shirts and having a great time in our booth when this guy came up and told me that his kids had learned their numbers by watching me count off sit-ups and push-ups on television while his wife worked out to the show. (Big Bird has nothing on me!)

"You seem to have a great rapport with kids. Have you ever thought about doing a family show?" he asked.

It just so happened I did. The *Big Brother Jake* show was built around my character, who returns to the foster home where he was raised to help his foster mother with five new kids.

It was really crowded at the booth, so I didn't have time to pitch my sitcom to him. I told him that I did have an idea for a kid's show and I'd be glad to talk to him about it after the convention. He gave me his card. I gave him my phone number and a couple of signed T-shirts for his kids.

"Call me if you are interested," I said.

It was a very quick conversation in a crowd of people. I didn't even know who the guy worked for until I looked at his card later. He was head of programming for The Family Channel. That sounded good but I wasn't sure that our brief conversation would lead anywhere. You collect a lot of business cards at NATPE, which is packed full of the television industry's movers and shakers—and people trying to pitch them on their ideas. It's the industry's biggest gathering, so you hear from a lot of people who want to do deals, but that doesn't mean they always follow through. This guy did.

When I got back to my office in L.A. on Monday, he called and invited me to come to the Family Channel's headquarters in Virginia Beach, Virginia, to talk about my series concept. I was pumped up. I'd been disappointed that the CBS deal fell through because having a regular television series is a lot of fun and, by the way, you can make some real dough! For me, it's like playing every day. So, I headed for Virginia Beach on the day he'd asked me to come. But when I got to the headquarters office of The Family Channel, my contact wasn't there.

I waited in the lobby for forty-five minutes. I was beginning to feel a little unloved when this casually dressed guy walks up and says, "Hey, aren't you the fitness guy?"

For some reason, I get that a lot.

I introduced myself and told this guy—"Tim"—that I was there to pitch a sitcom concept to The Family Channel's program chief.

"Well, he should be here any minute. Good luck," he said before wandering off.

Another twenty minutes went by without a word from the programming guy. I'd about given up on Virginia Beach when Tim came out again.

"You're still out here?" he said. "I'm sorry. There must have been a mix-up. Why don't you come into my office and tell me about your show."

I still had no idea who Tim was. But at that point, I didn't feel like wasting any more time describing my show to some junior executive. I told him that I could wait for the programming chief. Tim insisted he'd like to hear about it. He seemed like a friendly, sharp guy, and by that time I was just ready to unload my pitch and get back to business in L.A.

We went into his office, which didn't appear to be an executive suite. It wasn't even a corner office. We talked sports and fitness for a couple minutes and I started to relax. Then he got to the point.

"Tell me the essence of the show," he said.

I gave him the pitch. He laughed in all the right places.

"Let's do it," he said.

"Well, I'd better talk to the guy in charge first and see if he goes for it," I said.

"I'm the guy in charge," Tim Robertson said.

I had no idea even then who he was, but I was starting to get a clue. He wasn't just the guy in charge of The Family Channel. He and his father owned the entire operation.

Two months later, we shot the pilot for *Big Brother Jake*, and The Family Channel gave me an initial order for twenty-two episodes. We ended up doing 100 episodes between 1990 and 1995, and it was one of the most enjoyable experiences I've ever had in the television business.

I got to be good friends with Tim Robertson. In 1993, when I told him that I thought the market was ripe for a television network devoted to fitness and health, he offered to back me financially. We launched FitTV and had such great success with it that when Fox Sports bought it five years later it had a value of $500 million!

Now you know why I think of Tim Robertson as the angel of all angels! It was only natural then, that after I'd spoken with Dave Morrow at Warrior Lacrosse about my idea for a major outdoor lacrosse league, I immediately went to Tim and told him about it. He interrupted me after ten minutes and said, "I'm in."

He is now a partner with Dave Morrow and me in Major League Lacrosse. It's been a challenging experience to start up a new professional sports league. We've poured more than a few million dollars into it, which was about what we expected to do in our first several years. Yet Tim, who now runs his own venture capital firm, Bay Shore Enterprises, has been there for me, willing to up the ante and do whatever it takes to back the dream.

We work as a team of equals. I got them pumped, and through great times and very tough times we have always stuck together. I've never had a relationship like that in business. We've never had a fight. We have great conversations. I'm not kidding you here. We are three guys from three totally different backgrounds but we really work well together. And that's a rare thing. I know that I can always count on Tim and Dave.

It's easy to be pals with your investors when a business is churning out cash, but a big undertaking like Major League Lacrosse tests the strength of your partnership and your personal relationships. When we have disagreed, we've always come together after talking it through. I only wish all street-smart entrepreneurs could have people like Tim and Dave in their corners. I've told you that owning a business built around your interests is a great way to live. I won't tell you that it's always easy. It's not, especially when it comes to rustling up the money to meet all of the challenges that come in the first few months and years. But if you do your homework and carefully select your source of financing, it makes all the blood, sweat and tears easier to handle.

> *The best way to attract financing is to be knee-deep in profits.*

Digging for dollars is one of the toughest parts of being a street-smart entrepreneur. But everybody has to do it and it's absolutely necessary to get your dream business up and running. Get yourself psyched up to meet this challenge. Tune the word "no" out of your hearing range. And always re-member this mantra handed down by ancient wise street-smart gurus over the centuries:

Don't Quit Until You've Got the Dough!

name it and claim it

I DIDN'T HAVE two broomsticks to rub together in my early days in Hollywood, but I was in great shape. I was weight training like a madman, trying to become a professional bodybuilder. I was buff, cut, and polished—Steinfeld in stone, if I do say so myself. And like some of the great legends in Hollywood, I was discovered while just walking around one day!

In the summer of 1978, I was living way out in suburban Northridge and driving every day to a gym in the promised land of Santa Monica, the Mecca of professional bodybuilders. One day, on my way back to my apartment after a workout, I stopped at a drug store to get some vitamins. I was walking down the aisle in my extra small t-shirt and a pair of workout shorts when a woman tapped me on the shoulder.

"Excuse me, can I ask you a question?" she said.

"Sure," I replied, thinking she wanted to know the best brand of multi-vitamins.

"Have you ever heard of the Village People?" she asked.

Whoa! Not your typical conversation ice-breaker.

"Well, I've heard the name, but I'm more of a Jethro Tull guy myself."

She smiled, but she didn't run away. "The Village People have a song called 'Macho Man' and, I hope you take this the right way, you ARE the Macho Man!"

I stuck my chest out, flexed my biceps and said in my deepest voice: "Why, thank you. Thank you very much."

"So, would you like to pose on stage with The Village People at their concert at the Santa Monica Civic Center?"

"Am I on *Candid Camera*?" I asked.

She shook her head and smiled again.

Visions of me striking a pose in front of 50,000 screaming women flew through my mind. It was my Sinatra dream come to life!

"Oh, by the way, they'll pay you a hundred dollars to do it!" she added.

"Can I get some tickets for my parents and little sister?" I asked.

"No problem," she said.

She then introduced herself as Susie Frank and handed me a business card that said she was head of "A&R"—that's Artists and Repertoire—at Casablanca Records. She told me to meet her at her office that afternoon to sign a contract and pick up the free tickets.

I hustled down to Casablanca Records for our meeting. Susie treated me like rock royalty. She introduced me to the president of the company, Neil Bogart. Disco diva Donna Summer was in his office so I got to meet her too! They were terrific to me. I think Donna checked me out as I left with a bag of Casablanca's hottest hits, a $100 bill, and front-row tickets for my folks and my sister Nancy, who was five years old then but a real music fan.

They told me the concert was a sellout. I was pumped! I called my parents back in Long Island: "I'm going to be on stage at a rock concert, posing for the audience! I got you tickets because I thought you wouldn't want to miss this!"

My parents, who were always very supportive, said they'd book a flight, and, of course, my little sister Nancy was thrilled! (My two brothers were off at summer camp, so they missed out.) The rest of the week passed in slo-mo but finally my big night arrived in the form of a stretch limousine. Casablanca sent the car for me, which was really great since I'd never been in one before. We cruised to the Santa Monica Civic Center, where the big sign said "The Village People concert is sold out!" I didn't see my name on the billboard, but that was okay. I got out, flashed my backstage pass at the security gate, and strolled in like one of the boys in the band.

A security guy took me to my own dressing room. I'd always dreamed about being backstage at a rock concert. It was very cool, though I was a little surprised that there didn't seem to be many girls hanging around. I figured maybe these Village People kept them out front until the show was over so they could focus on the music. I peeked out at the audience to check out the crowd and look for my parents and sister. They'd taken all of the seats out and turned the whole place into a giant disco floor! I couldn't see much of the crowd because the lights were in my eyes but I was getting psyched about posing in front of thousands of screaming ladies!

I went to my dressing room, took off my sweats, and rubbed in the Baby Oil so my muscles would shine in the lights. I was wearing just my little posing trunks under a robe, feeling like a greased watermelon. They had me stay there until near the end of the show for the big Macho Man finale. Finally, they called my name and told me to stand behind the curtain. When the stage director waved me over to a spot just behind the curtain, I heard one of the guys in the band say: "How many of you out there think you are macho men? Well, we have somebody tonight who is really macho. Come on out, Jake!"

The stage director sent me out just as the group started singing "Macho, macho man . . ."

As soon as I hit the stage there was this big roar from the crowd. It was a rush! I flexed a bicep. They roared twice as loud!

I did a couple more quick poses and the crowd went into a frenzy! So this is what it feels like to be Mick Jagger, I thought.

Finally, I worked my way front and center and looked out for the first time into the audience to find my proud parents and sister. I couldn't believe my eyes! My Dad, Mom, and little sister were standing there with these mortified, deer-in-the-headlights looks on their faces. It hit me why when I looked at the crowd around them. It was all guys! Thousands of them, and they were waving white hankies. At me! They were also blowing kisses. At me! And making other gestures that I won't go into. At me!

Suddenly, it dawned on me that the Village People had a unique following—not that there is anything wrong with that. It just wasn't what I'd expected. It obviously wasn't what my father, mother, and sister had expected either. As soon as the song was over, I rushed backstage, threw on my sweats and got out of there. My parents met me in the parking lot. My father was pale. My mother and sister looked at me as if to say, *What were you thinking?*

My father, who was a man of few words, only uttered four words: "Go back to college!"

And that brings us to the topic of this chapter: *Street-smart brand management.*

The Boys and the Brand

Appearing on stage with The Village People was definitely a trip for a former fat kid who stuttered and couldn't get up in front of his grade school class to read. It was a strange experience, but something I'll never forget. As it turned out, the guys in The Village People were very nice to me and my parents after the show, and we have laughed about it many times since. It was one of those "youthful" experiences that I'd probably never do again, especially now that I have a global brand to think about.

| *Your reputation is your most important business asset!*

Today, I spend nearly every waking business hour thinking about guarding, building and expanding on the *Body By Jake* brand, and the Major League Lacrosse brand too. I'm always getting calls from people who want me to endorse their products, but I'm very careful about what I attach my name to. I've got a brand of my own to protect. When you get down to it, the most important thing you own is the reputation and public image of your business, its products, and Y-O-U, too!

Before I started *Body By Jake*, I had only the typical awareness of what brands were or how important they are. I mean, I ate Cheerios. I drank Coca-Cola. I wanted a Chevy Corvette. I knew those were brand names but

I didn't give it much thought. But as a street-smart entrepreneur, you need to give a whole lot of thought and commitment to creating, building, and expanding your brand and its image in the marketplace. Your brand isn't just the name of your company or the names of its products or services. It's what connects you to the hearts, minds, guts and souls of your customers.

Think about it. When you hear Starbucks do you think just of coffee? No, you think of sitting in a comfortable chair, listening to great music, talking with friends, reading the newspaper or getting online, AND sipping a double tall dry cappuccino with a little milk and a lot of foam (my favorite!). That's the power of a brand versus a simple product or company name.

The most successful brands create an experience and a relationship with customers or clients. Every great brand has a unique, appealing and thoughtfully created personality all its own.

BMW? *It's a driving/lifestyle experience!*

Apple's iPod? *Cutting edge, cool high-tech living!*

Louis Vuitton? *Accessories for a life in high fashion!* (According to my wife, that is.)

The power of those brands is based on how they make their customers feel about themselves and the relationship they develop with them. Amazon .com pioneered this approach for Web entrepreneurs by creating an entire culture for its regular customers. Using sophisticated tracking methods, it looks at their purchases to get a handle on each individual's tastes and then presents each customer with suggested purchases every time someone logs on to its Web site. It's the modern equivalent of good salesmanship. In the old days, the corner dress shop owner might have called her best customers to tell them when she was having a sale or when a new shipment of the latest fashions has arrived. Today, it's Amazon.com building its brand relationships by welcoming customers with book and music recommendations based on their previous purchases. That's not just Web smart. It's street smart!

| *Brands are built on customer satisfaction!*

The new Internet movie rental Web site, Netflix, is another example of a brand-smart company that's been very astute about building relationships with customers. Netflix has grown quickly because it provides such good service that more than 90 percent of its customers bring in more new clients. The Netflix Web site encourages customers to communicate with each other about their favorite movies, which helps build a brand community. Netflix has also worked hard to build more than twenty-four distribution centers around the country so people don't have to wait more than a day or two to get the movies they order.

Customer service and community building are hallmarks of another great brand, Apple Computers. When Apple founder Steve Jobs introduces a new product to his customers, he usually does it in some giant convention hall where they gather by the thousands. It's like an evangelical service with people cheering and whooping it up because over the years, Apple has delivered great products to its loyal fans. They are devoted to his brand. He's a great brand builder even though he's had to fight for his company and his vision over the years.

| Get creative with your brand.

You've got to have that same toughness and commitment in building and managing your company's brand. It will take guts to stick with your vision and keep proving yourself time and again. Steve Jobs even lost control of his own company for a time before he staged an incredible comeback. Today, Apple is kicking buttissimo with its iTunes and iPod products. To build a great brand like that you've got to have a very clear vision of what your customers or clients want and need. You've go to create a bond with them and you've got to stand by your products or services. Great brand building calls for creativity, not just in the beginning but throughout the life of your company.

My guess is that at this point you are thinking: This brand-building stuff sounds like it costs more than you can afford. Excuse me. I'm the guy who told you at the beginning of this chapter that I didn't have two broomsticks to rub together when I started out. But guess what? Even if you have no money in the bank, you can build your brand with creativity.

In the early 1980s, a visionary Atlanta entrepreneur with a start-up news network saw a *People* magazine story about my fitness-training success with the Hollywood elite. Ted Turner tracked me down and said he thought I could help him make his Cable News Network more viewer-friendly. I had never heard of his network, so I didn't exactly jump at the opportunity. I checked out CNN and Ted with friends in television and they said both of them were wild cards. Nobody gave CNN much of a chance of surviving competition from the networks, but a few people I talked to said they thought Ted was a maverick genius who just might be on to something.

It struck me that Turner's national network offered the opportunity to promote my brand and maybe help my acting career too. I called him back and suggested doing 60-second vignettes as "fitness breaks" that he could run throughout the 24-hour cycle of his network. He liked the idea because it was low-cost programming that provided real value to his viewers. It turned out to be a great thing for both his network and for my career. Those spots on CNN were 60-second commercials for my brand, and Ted was paying me to do them! My CNN spots opened the door to unbelievable opportunities. They ran and ran and ran on CNN, giving me more exposure than Wolf Blitzer. In our first three-day shoot, we did 200 vignettes at locations in Malibu, Beverly Hills, and the Hollywood Hills. Over the next four years, we shot another 800 vignettes.

Back then, no one knew whether CNN would last a week. But my willingness to do the work for minimum wages, led to lucrative deals for home videos, exercise books, hundreds of personal appearances, my own television series and, eventually, my own television network, which was purchased for more money than I'd ever dreamed of having.

Are you getting this? I don't have a college education. I moved to L.A. with a potted plant and a stack of bodybuilding magazines. And I built a solid, dependable and customer-friendly brand!

One more thing: I've got NOTHING on you! It doesn't take a college degree, or a boatload of money. All it takes is commitment to your own street-smart success!

| *Build trust by delivering on the promise.*

To this day, much of my success traces back to those CNN days of brand-building and the exposure it gave me and my young brand. Corporations spend millions and millions building, promoting, and protecting their brands to maintain power in the marketplace. *Business Week* named the world's most valuable global brands among companies with $1 billion or more in sales. The names are familiar, of course, but what's interesting is that these companies were selected based on their future earning potential because of the long-term strength of their brands. You don't see brand-building in fly-by-night operations. But if you want your business to have long-term success, you create, grow and manage your brand as thoughtfully as these giant companies. It takes time to build your brand and you can't buy trust. That is why you have to build your brand organically. These monster brands spend billions of dollars marketing and promoting their products, but you want to make sure that you build trust by delivering on the promise of your business.

Business Week's Top Ten Global Brands

1. COCA-COLA

2. MICROSOFT

3. IBM

4. GE

5. INTEL

6. DISNEY

7. McDONALD'S

8. NOKIA

9. TOYOTA

10. MARLBORO

Street-Smart Tips for Building Your Brand

1. BUILD A BRAND BASE

In bodybuilding, when you start to train you start light and build a foundation of strength so your body knows how to react to different exercises. You build muscle memory. Once you've got that base, the potential is unlimited. It works the same way with your company and its brand. Great brands like those cited by *Business Week* stand up over time because they've developed extremely loyal, sometimes even fanatic, followings. All of the companies in that top ten list, including Coca-Cola and Disney, have had challenges in recent years, but because they have such a strong base, they are able to weather the rocky times and still find new ways to build on their brands and continue to generate new streams of revenue.

The secret is to create a brand that isn't just about a product or service, it's about a way of life that generates excitement and enthusiasm. And it's about being, as they say at Coke, "the real thing." If you expect your customers or clients to stick with you through thick and thin, you'd better be straight with them from the start. We do everything but crash-test our *Body By Jake* fitness products into walls at 50 miles per hour just to make certain that they live up to and reinforce our reputation for reliable, solid, easy-to-use equipment. People expect that from us, and we are determined not to disappoint them. It's not easy building a strong brand base, but it's absolutely necessary because today's consumers don't mess around.

> *Build a brand that isn't just about a product or service; make it a way of life.*

Once people decided they wanted to eat healthier, they began demanding that fast-food companies get the fat out. Subway listened, and as a result that franchise has thrived while many others have struggled. Today's brands have to be stand-up, or consumers will knock them down. So you'd better build your company and your brand on solid ground by setting high standards from top to bottom.

Coca-Cola is the world's most recognized and respected brand. The Atlanta-based soft-drink company pioneered brand management around the globe, and it also has fought to protect its brand. Coke has used undercover "Coke spies" to visit soft-drink retailers to make sure that when someone orders a Coke they get the "real thing." Keep in mind that when you create a brand you've got to be prepared to defend it around the world in today's global market. Even Coca-Cola faces challenges constantly and not just from its arch-rival Pepsi.

One of the latest Coke challengers is Mecca Cola. Named after the holiest place in the Islamic world, its creators are taking cola wars to a whole new realm by advising its target market to reject American products with the slogan: "Don't drink stupid. Drink with commitment." Mecca Cola, which comes in a familiar-looking red can with white script lettering, was introduced in France a couple years ago by a Tunisian guy looking to capitalize on anti-American sentiments in the Middle East.

> *When you create a brand in today's global market, be prepared to defend it around the world.*

I'm not sure how well global politics and soda pop mix, but there is already a diet version of Mecca Cola as well as apple-, lime-, and orange-flavored drinks produced by the same company and exported throughout Europe and the Arab world. Of course, you won't see Mecca Cola being used as a mixer with rum or other alcoholic beverages. There's fine print on the bottle that says mixing it with alcohol is against the Islamic religion.

The in-your-face challenge to Coke from Mecca Cola is a reminder that in a global economy, you've got to build a brand base that's strong enough to take on a whole world of competition. That's why branding a business is about more than just trying to get your customers to slap their money down for your product or service. As a street-smart entrepreneur you want to win their hearts and minds too.

The brand strength of the Walt Disney Company also has been tested in recent years with management upheaval, criticism of its top executives and board of directors, and a hostile takeover threat. Yet, even as all of that was going on, this great American company hardly broke stride because of the strength of its beloved brand and its place in the hearts of the world. They may still have some work to do at Disney, but the company has proven the power of its brand in recent years.

Even once-strong brands that have lost their way can stage dramatic recoveries if they have strong enough bonds with consumers. Just look at the Ford Mustang. It staged an incredible comeback in 2005 primarily because when all was said and done, people have a strong gut feeling about the car that was truly America's first affordable sports car.

2. MAKE IT AN EXPERIENCE

Warrior Lacrosse is one of the hottest new brands in the country because its creator understands the importance of building a brand with a strong base—*and* of creating an entire experience around it. That's something that I admired about Dave Morrow when I first talked to him about launching Major League Lacrosse. He and his wife Christine had already worked hard to build Warrior Lacrosse into a youthful brand that people want to be a part of because it conveys a cutting edge, fun lifestyle. Sure, the company's primary products were lacrosse equipment and sportswear, but he'd packaged the brand as a lifestyle so it was positioned for expansion into all sorts of things.

I wasn't the only street-smart guy who noticed the power of his Warrior Lacrosse brand. Not long after Dave and I partnered up with Tim Robertson to start Major League Lacrosse, he received a great offer from another very savvy entrepreneur, Jim Davis, chairman and CEO of New Balance, the global maker of performance athletic footwear. Jim and Dave had partnered in creating the "Warrior Burn," a high-performance shoe for lacrosse players designed in consultation with the best players in the game. When they worked together on the shoe's design, Jim saw that Dave had tapped into a hot market. Like me, Jim saw that lacrosse is one of the country's fastest growing sports. He also recognized that the Warrior Lacrosse brand was very popular with young athletes who fit into the same demographic as New Balance's target market.

In fact, Jim and his team at New Balance in Boston got so excited about the Warrior Lacrosse brand and Dave Morrow's vision for it that they wrote a check for millions to buy the company and keep Dave as its president. I think that's a pretty strong statement of belief in the power of a brand, don't you? Here's what Jim Davis had to say about Warrior's brand when he announced that New Balance had purchased the company:

> Warrior is original, young, energetic, and unafraid of creating changes that can lead into uncharted territory. It is a distinct expression of the ambition, creativity, and will of founder and president Dave Morrow, a former champion lacrosse player.

Do me a favor. No, do yourself and your business a favor and read that paragraph again. Think about how it would feel one day to have the president and CEO of a billion-dollar company say that about your street-smart start-up? Regardless of whether it comes with a check for many millions, that sort of statement would be golden to me and to most entrepreneurs because it recognizes that you've built not just a company but a powerful brand too!

What's a brand worth? After all, it's just a name right?

Wrong! Zap!

New Balance didn't pay millions for a small and young company that makes equipment for lacrosse players. The price was that high because Jim Davis bought into the power of the Warrior Lacrosse brand! Dave Morrow built not just a company but a brand with unlimited potential by creating not just sporting equipment but an experience too.

Dave Morrow didn't spend millions on advertising to promote Warrior Lacrosse. Instead, he marketed to the young, hip, and athletic crowd and let *them* sell his products and brand appeal through word of mouth and by, well, just showing up with his gear. Call it guerilla marketing, call it street smart, call it a shot to the net for a major win by one great guy and his powerful brand. Now, it's your turn to take a shot!

3. WIN THE BRAND LOYALTY OF YOUR MARKET

So how do you build the same sort of brand value for your company that Dave Morrow created at Warrior Lacrosse? Well, I think you've got to be a brand warrior yourself! You've got to champion the cause and lead the charge into the market. But mostly, you've got to believe in it yourself! That's right. When you get right down to it, your business brand is a measure of how much pride you take in what you do, how much you believe in your own product or services, and how willing you are to do whatever it takes to stand by and to deliver on the promise to your customers or clients.

At *Body By Jake*, we've commissioned a bunch of studies that show the power of having an established and respected industry brand around the world. When you get right down to it, our most important asset is the strong reputation of our brand and the trust that it inspires in our customers. We've got a lot of great people and great products, but it's the brand's lifestyle that people buy into.

> *Be willing to do whatever it takes to build trust with your customers.*

I didn't invent the sit-up or push-up, but my first clients came to trust in me and my training methods, and in my ability to motivate them in ways that were entertaining and encouraging.

Today, the *Body By Jake* brand has that same, very intimate relationship with our customers. It's that way, in part, because when people watch me on infomercials or the Home Shopping Network, most of them are at home either getting up or going to bed in their pajamas. It's fascinating because it really becomes a very personal relationship between them and the brand. They come to trust our products because they trust me, and I don't want to disappoint them because they buy our products without touching or testing them. So there has to be trust, or they won't buy into our promises. I've got to tell you, it makes me proud that people trust in me and the *Body By Jake* brand. That relationship is one of the greatest things about being in business!

My company has grown from a groundbreaking, one-man fitness training business into a global brand that we now have to be very careful and thoughtful about managing. One of the things we've been real happy about is that *Body By Jake* fitness products are regarded as easy to operate, durable, and reliable. I'm not just tooting the BBJ horn here. Our focus groups and customer surveys all say that our products deliver on the promise. If you buy them and use them properly, they work!

We talk a lot about building abs, pecs, and biceps, but our biggest strength at *Body By Jake* is the connection our customers have with our brand. They feel like part of our family, and we regard them in that way. It's a business, sure, and we're in it to make money, but we're also in it to provide something worthwhile to the people who put their trust in us by buying our products. Since we sincerely feel that way about them, they feel the same way about us. Our surveys and focus group reports say that *Body By Jake* is seen as a company that encourages a fun, fit lifestyle that is supportive but not intimidating. We offer easy, affordable "real life" fitness solutions that anyone can use to attain a healthier life. We also promote our company as a supportive partner that helps gives its customers a new sense of purpose and power over their lives.

As I was putting this book together, we produced a new infomercial for our Ab Scissor product. It was the first time we'd done a second show for a product, but we had gotten so many great e-mails, letters, and phone calls that we decided to do an infomercial in which our customers were the stars. We put out the word that we were interested in having people who were using the Ab Scissor on the new infomercials. I couldn't believe how many people responded. More than 60,000 customers contacted us saying they wanted to tell their stories! Phenomenal! (I get teary-eyed just thinking about it. You love me, you really, really love me!)

Seriously, that sort of brand loyalty is money in the bank, but it's even better than that. It's what gets me up in the morning and keeps me going every day. I've got to believe in what I'm selling. I thrive on the fact that my business improves the lives of our customers. I want you to have that same tremendous pride for your business, whatever it is, because you can't expect your customers to love it if you don't.

When you look at some of the most successful and dynamic newer brands out there, like Starbucks and Southwest Airlines, you can feel the enthusiasm from the top people all the way down to the those on the front lines. Another one of my favorite brands is ESPN, the Sports Network, and not just because it televises Major League Lacrosse. I've had a long relationship with ESPN dating back to our early days when I did my fitness show for them. It's interesting because when former sportscaster Bill Rassmussen and his son Scott started ESPN back in 1979, a lot of naysayers made fun of them. Remember, this was before there were any 24-hour networks of any kind out there—not CNN, not HBO, not MTV! The Rassmussens' critics said nobody would watch or advertise on an all-sports, all-the-time network. Remember that you'll no doubt hear the same sort of baloney. I heard it when I launched FitTV, and I'm still hearing it as Major League Lacrosse prepares for its fifth season. So it's great to still be doing business with ESPN and the powerful brand they created, even though the Rassmussens sold out in 1984 and it's now owned by The Walt Disney Company, the ABC network, and the Hearst Corporation.

| *Treat 'em like royalty and you'll win their loyalty!*

Today at ESPN they have more than 88 million viewers. Their top executives talk constantly about "fanning the flames" in their relationship with their viewers and other customers and fans. Maybe I get along with them so well because we have similar philosophies. Their CEO, George Bodenheime, is a friend of mine. He's an awesome guy, who has built ESPN into a global giant. He's also a great family man and a true believer in creating business and personal relationships based on trust.

ESPN is interesting because of their philosophy of taking sports very seriously, but not taking themselves that seriously. It's an international conglomerate with the feel of a great sports club in which the members or customers come first. That's a good way to build a brand, by serving the interests and needs of your customers. ESPN keeps its brand focused and true to its roots by always remembering that the founding father and son were fans who were passionate about the concept of a 24-hour sports, news, and information network.

It goes back to believing in your own brand. If you are passionate about your business, it's sure to fan the flames of your target audience. It's sure worked for ESPN. You probably don't realize it, but it is now a major global corporation with forty different businesses, including twenty-five television networks—ESPN, ESPN2, ESPN Classic, ESPNEWS, ESPN Deportes, ESPN Today, ESPN HD, ESPN Regional Television, and ESPN International. They also have ESPN Radio, ESPN.com, ESPN The Magazine, SportsTicker, ESPN Enterprises, ESPN Zone restaurants, ESPN Broadband, ESPN Wireless, ESPN Video-on-Demand, ESPN Interactive, and ESPN Pay Per View.

Look for ways to give your customer more bang for the buck!

When you are looking to grow your business and expand the brand, it's always a good idea to "check the connection" with your customers and clients by looking at whether these new endeavor serves their interests. At *Body By Jake*, we always look at new opportunities in that light. Is it true to our overall mission to build a business around a healthy and fit lifestyle? Does it offer our loyal customers more value and more opportunities to improve the quality of their lives? ESPN asks similar questions. For George Bodenheimer's company, it's all about serving the fans.

Get your customers to buy into your brand.

As a street-smart entrepreneur, you've got to take your brand or brands just as seriously as your customers do—and believe me, they do. The global advertising firm Saatchi & Saatchi tracks how people feel about their favorite brands at a Web site called Lovemarks.com. It's a strange place where thousands of people write love letters to their favorite brands, like Abercrombie & Fitch, Wonder Bread, BMW, Budweiser, Slurpees, and Oshkosh By Gosh (no relation to *Body By Jake*, just the same middle name). You should check it out just to see for yourself how important it is to create a true relationship with your customers or clients through your brand.

When your customers or clients have an emotional attachment to your brand, they are more likely to snap up your products as soon as they hear about them. I see this firsthand when I appear on Home Shopping Network.

Their computer monitoring system shows me that our loyal customers who've come to trust our brand will pick up the phone and order new offerings. Apple has discovered this with iTunes and the iPod.

Brain scientist Donald Calne offers scientific proof from his studies, noting that the main difference between emotion and reason is that "Emotion leads to action, while reason leads to conclusion." When you build a trusting long-term relationship with your customers through your brand, it helps them make buying decisions more quickly. It's important to first build trust in your brand and then work to seal the bond by building direct bridges to your customer through Internet Web sites, mailings, and any other ways you can reach out to them and stay in touch.

4. GO BROAD BRAND

The most successful companies are careful not to build their brand around just one product. Even a global leader like Coca-Cola, which is primarily known for Coke, is constantly looking for ways to expand the brand with other spin-off products and related soft drinks and snacks. The legendary company's brand managers promote each of the products as part of a healthy, active lifestyle. Their introduction of a global advertising campaign for the Athens 2004 Olympics is typical of Coke's brand management philosophy:

> The Coca-Cola Company believes the Olympic Games are the place where the best of human nature is shown. We also believe that Coca-Cola is the brand that best captures the spirit of genuine moments in life. Together, the Olympics and Coca-Cola celebrate the very best of humanity, and together, we believe in a better world.

While Coca-Cola is the main brand, the company owns more than 400 others, including A&W Root Beer, POWERADE, Hi-C, Fresca, Fruitopia, and Limonade. In China, Coke offers *Tian Yu Di* ("Heaven and Earth") for "young urban adults who want bottled water with unmatched thirst-quenching ability."

We've done the same thing with our *Body By Jake* brand. It's not associated with just one product. It's about living a healthier, more active and more focused life. That overall "lifestyle" brand allows us to grow by continually launching new and different types of products while still maintaining our image.

Going with this broad brand approach also prevents your company or business from being too closely identified with you or any other individual. In some circles, they call this the *Martha Stewart Syndrome.* I don't take pleasure in anyone's misfortunes, and so I don't like that term, but her case does illustrate a point. She is a great entrepreneur but when she had troubles with the IRS and went through a high profile trial, her company and all of its employees and stockholders suffered because the business was so closely identified with its founder and guiding force. You've got to give Martha credit, though. Thanks to a solid foundation, her business and her company bounced back even before she'd completed her sentence.

I've done the same. My model for building a stand-alone business may seem like an unlikely one given our very different lines of work, but I think the legendary Beverly Hills hairstylist Vidal Sassoon did a very street-smart thing. Like me, Vidal originally became known for working with celebrities in Hollywood. He became a global pioneer in his industry after starting with one salon. He developed a respected brand in his image by serving as its spokesman, and then, very gradually, faded into the background by using younger people in his commercials and ads. That was very shrewd brand-marketing because it allows his company to keep growing beyond his involvement. Vidal Sassoon is a great branding role model. I call his calculated fade from the public forefront of his brand, the "Sassoon swoon." And some day, I might do my own version of it so that my sons and daughter will be able to step in and run the company, if that's what they want to do.

My name—and body too—are closely linked to the company and its image because *Body By Jake* began as a one-man operation. It just naturally evolved that way, but as the company has grown, we've realized that the brand needs to grow too. So rather than have to change the name to *Body By Jake Jr.* (not that there is a Jake Jr., but I do have four kids now), we've worked to promote *Body By Jake* products without my image. Down the road, we will be using other spokespeople just to broaden the brand a little more. We are now developing *Body By Jake* Master Trainers who can serve as spokespeople. We've also worked to broaden the brand. In both of our Ab Scissor infomercials we've done a spot with NFL and Major League Baseball star Deion Sanders and his wife Pilar, a beautiful model, because their endorsements help us reach an even wider audience. One day, *Body By Jake* might even offer a line of fitness equipment bearing the brands of other great physical specimens, like Deion and Pilar Sanders.

For my company to endure, we have to develop other product lines with their own brands. We're going to look at growing your business in the next chapter, but keep in mind that expanding the brand is a very important way to open new markets, create fresh opportunities, and grow.

5. BE THE BRAND!

So far, I've given you tips on branding for your business and its products or services. Yet, I want you to remember that it all starts with you, the street-smart entrepreneur. You will never build brand loyalty and convince your customers or clients that your products are honest, reliable and dependable if you don't live and conduct your business that way too. You've got to be the brand—one that you'd want to buy into yourself.

If you find your company struggling in its early days—maybe customers aren't calling or coming in the door—the first thing you should check is the state of your own brand. When you aren't getting what you want out of life, don't blame your circumstances or other people. Check yourself first. Maybe your own brand recognition is out of whack. Take a look at what you represent as a person. Have you proven yourself as a reliable, honest, helpful person who adds value to family, friends, neighbors, and customers or clients? You can have the greatest product on earth, but if people don't buy into you, they won't come shopping at your business.

| *Live up to your brand image.*

Your personal brand is more important than those you stamp on your products or services as an entrepreneur. So think about what you represent in your field and community as well as in your relationships. You build your personal brand by identifying values and principles to guide your life and the critical decisions you have to make along the way. If you don't understand that, your customers will make it abundantly clear at some point. You've got to live it to give it. I've worked hard to build a brand that offers family-oriented health and fitness products.

When you create a brand image for your products or services and then forge a relationship with your customer, they expect you to live up to it. If you don't, they'll take their loyalties somewhere else. So don't throw all your hard work away. Once you've built a bond with your customers, live up to their brand expectations. Or be ready to pay the consequences.

I'm not suggesting that you live a lie, or that you build your life around other people's expectations. Instead, I'm advising you to set the same high standards for your business that you set for yourself.

Not long ago, we were in a deal with an infomercial company that had come up with a fitness product that I really liked. But before I would allow them to put my name on it, I asked them to improve the quality of its materials and construction. They agreed to make all the changes. They even built a prototype to match my specifications for it. So, we gave them the green light. We were happy with the changes to the point that we went ahead and shot an infomercial for the product. But we didn't see the first of the new and improved models until we'd completed the infomercial and we were shocked at what we discovered. They were not up to my standards in any way. The infomercial producer had not been straight with me. They'd skimped on the quality of the materials and construction. So, I walked away from the deal.

Fortunately for us, we were still a licensing company at that point so we didn't have a lot of money invested, but it hurt nonetheless. Still, I didn't think we could afford to send out products that didn't live up to the brand's reputation and risk damaging our relationship with our customers.

I believe that the companies I create are part of who I am. They aren't "just businesses." They are a reflection of my values and my integrity. I have many loyal customers because they understand that about me. They know I'm a stand-up guy who stands behind his products. I believe you are what you sell. If you want people to value your reputation and your brand, then you'd better have high standards for whatever product or service you put out there. You will find that when you set the bar high for yourself and for your business, the rewards will come both in personal satisfaction and in customer loyalty. So, be the brand!

growing strong

YOU COULD HAVE knocked me down with a Flowbee when I first heard
the word come out of the mouth of Phil Scotti, president of *Body By Jake*,
back in 1992.

"Infomercials? Are you nuts, Philly?"

To be fair, Phil was only repeating what one of our equipment manufacturing partners had brought up a few minutes earlier. But I'd just thrown
him out a window. (He landed softly, don't worry).

I couldn't toss Phil. He had a company insurance policy. Still, I was
shocked that he'd even consider selling one of our fitness products on an
infomercial.

But Phil said, "Jake, if we could do it your way, we could make the
infomercial format work for us." Infomercials first hit the airwaves in 1984
after the Federal Communications Commission lifted its restrictions on how
much television time had to be devoted to actual programming. The first
true hour-long infomercial was really just an extended commercial. It was
for an Herbalife weight-loss supplement. Mark Hughes, the founder of

Herbal Life, was one of my training clients in the mid-1980s. He was a supersalesman who lived very large (I teased him that he lived like Elvis), and his business empire spanned the globe. I also told him one day that he should add a fitness component to his weight loss programs. A few days later, he presented me with a blank check saying he wanted to buy *Body By Jake* and make my workout program part of his company. It was tempting, but I remember thinking back then that I would never sell my name, or my brand, to another company and lose control of it.

I've always felt that I had to protect my brand as carefully as I'd protect my personal reputation. That's why I was wary of doing infomercials at first.

"Why would we want to go there?" I asked Phil.

"We wouldn't go there," he said. "You could do infomercials your way."

Phil always gets to me by quoting the ultimate street-smart guy: Sinatra. He made the point that infomercials offered a great opportunity to grow our business by marketing our products directly to consumers—if we could do it with a whole lot more class. One of the greatest strengths of the *Body By Jake* brand is the trust that our customers have in me and our products. Doing a special kind of infomercial seemed like a way to strengthen that bond, and so I agreed with Phil that infomercials might be worth a try if we could do them in a classier way. In 1992, we partnered with USA Direct, an infomercial producer, to do our first thirty-minute show. The featured product was our FirmFlex, the first home fitness machine designed to work the whole body without using weight stacks. The infomercial taped in front of a studio audience was built around a complete twenty-minute daily workout, with seven exercises called "the Simple Seven."

I'm a lot more comfortable doing infomercials now, but I think I did a pretty darn good job for my first shot at it. After all, I'd already done hundreds of Fitness Breaks for CNN and thirty-minute shows on ESPN, so I'd had a lot of time in front of the camera by then. I was also doing my own sit-com at that time. In fact, I had to fly to Los Angeles to do the infomercial in a small Hollywood studio during a break in taping the *Big Brother Jake* series on The Family Channel in Virginia Beach. It was an interesting experience because something else really important was going on at the time. My wife Tracey was pregnant with our first child. As soon as I got back from doing the infomercial, we went to the hospital and our daughter Morgan was born! Talk about a big production!

The Firm Flex infomercial was nearly as big a hit as Morgan. We sold more than 600,000 units. It became the top-selling fitness machine in the country—and the customer satisfaction rating was 98 percent! We did it our way, and it worked better than we could have imagined. Better yet, this new way of marketing *Body By Jake* products helped our business take a giant leap forward in growth. It changed everything!

Today, infomercials are a $154 billion business around the world. They are such an effective and successful way to grow business that companies such as General Motors, Kodak, Mercedes-Benz, Discover Card, and others are producing their own programs. *Body By Jake* is recognized as a pioneer and standard-setter in infomercial production. We now spend around a half-million dollars to produce our own infomercials on location in Hawaii and other great places. We also spend more than $20 million each year buying television time to air them around the country. Producing and marketing our own infomercials has turned out to be a major force for growth in our business. And like so many other great growth opportunities, it has led to even more opportunities, such as the Home Shopping Network.

We've been doing HSN for more than ten years now, and I've got to tell you, I've really come to love it! It's show business. It's the retail business and it's the people business all rolled into one fantastic experience. It used to be that owning your own store on the town square was the only way you could market your products directly to your customers and sell them at the same time. Not anymore! When I step in front of the cameras at HSN, I'm instantly connected to millions and millions of viewers and I can actually see and feel that connection because the studio has monitors linked to their phone and computer systems. The monitors show how many calls are coming in during our HSN shows and how many sales are being racked up while I'm on the air!

We also take calls from viewers and customers during the show so I can actually talk to them and get their feedback just as if I was on the floor of the *Body By Jake* store on Main Street USA! It is fan-tastic! And our partnership with HSN has been very, very, very good to both of our businesses. We are one of their premiere partners, selling millions of dollars in equipment over the past ten years on their stages. Now, I know that most small business owners probably can't afford to do infomercials or appear on the Home Shopping Network in the first few years of their companies' existence, but I encourage you to take responsibility and control of the growth of your street-smart business by looking for innovative and more effective ways to get your product or services out there. You can do it too!

Good to Grow

Being in control of my own destiny is one of the biggest reasons I enjoy being an entrepreneur. The same is true for most street-smart entrepreneurs and, I hope, for you too. To stay in control of your business, you need to be aware that if you aren't looking for innovative ways to grow it, you're running the risk of losing it.

| *You've got to grow to stay in the flow!*

Each week, month, and year that you remain in business will bring new opportunities for growth. Growing your revenues is essential because you can bet that your costs are going to increase too. It will seem like every month brings new costs and expenses for things like taxes, employees, materials, supplies, and essentials like electricity, fuel, and property rent. Small business owners typically say their biggest concerns are generating fresh revenue streams, dealing with rising insurance costs and, of course, staying ahead of the competition.

If you aren't actively working to grow your business, you'll lose out to competitors who are more aggressive and faster on their feet. Don't get me wrong, I think competition is good. Having a strong competitor should make your business healthier and stronger if you have the right attitude about it. Many of the people I worked with in Hollywood are very competitive, which isn't surprising when you consider how tough it is to succeed in the entertainment business. Most struggled and fought for years to become stars or top executives, and they have had to fight hard to stay on top once they got there.

Even one of the most bankable leading men, Harrison Ford, had to work hard for his success. He's a regular guy, whose drive and determination made him one of the most successful, long-term stars in Hollywood. When I was training Harrison to get him in shape for his second Indiana Jones role, in *Indiana Jones and the Temple of Doom*, we got to be good buddies. Harrison was a late bloomer. He wasn't a big athlete as a kid. The guy who has saved the United States of America and entire galaxies as an action movie hero was a member of the audio-visual and model railroad clubs, and the social science club at Park Ridge High School in Chicago. Harrison dropped out of college, then took some acting classes and moved to Hollywood hoping to make it as an actor. In his first role, he played a bellman who disappeared from the movie once he handed a telegram to the star, James Coburn. He had a hard time getting regular work as an actor but he kept going to casting calls. "They tried to kill me off with poisons, sharp sticks and blunt objects and I was like a snake that grew a new tail," he once said of those days.

Since Harrison had to pay the bills and support a family, he decided to look for other work when he wasn't getting any roles. He'd always been a handy guy, so he went to the library, read everything he could on carpentry, and started a new career. He built a recording studio for musician Sergio Mendes, a sundeck for actress Sally Kellerman, and bookcases for authors John Gregory Dunne and Joan Didion. I was the fitness trainer to the stars, and Harrison was their Hollywood handyman.

I got to know him when Steven Spielberg asked me to train Harrison during the filming of *The Temple of Doom*. While he was doing push-ups, I'd count them off faster and faster until he gave me a glare and called me things that would never get into a family movie. But he also kept doing the push-ups just to prove that I couldn't break him or beat him. He's a very competitive guy. One day after filming on location in London, Harrison threw his Indiana Jones fedora, leather jacket, and whip into the trunk of a rented car and asked me if I wanted to ride back to the hotel with him. On the way, he suggested we stop at a pub for a drink. I thought it would be fun to see how the Brits would respond to a movie star in their midst. When we walked into the packed pub, the patrons all looked up immediately, but it wasn't Harrison they were staring at, it was me. Finally, one little guy spoke up:

"Aren't you an American footballer?" he asked.

It just happened that two NFL teams were staging a pre-season exhibition game in London's Wembley Stadium that weekend and, since I was a pumped-up American guy, they thought I was from one of the teams. Before I could set them straight, they started bombarding me with questions about the sport so I just went with the flow. Everyone gathered around me, and so I offered to buy a round of drinks. I looked to see whether Harrison wanted to join in on the fun but he was nowhere to be seen. I figured he'd ditched me. But a few minutes later, out of the corner of my eye I saw a figure standing near the door.

It was Harrison. He'd gone back to the car and grabbed his movie star gear. He was standing there in his Indiana Jones hat! I had a bunch of drinks in my hand for the football fans, but there was nobody standing around me. As they surrounded him, Harrison looked at me with the glow of victory in his eyes! I reminded him later that he had to "go Hollywood" to steal the limelight from me.

Competition keeps me pumped up, and you should welcome it too as a street-smart entrepreneur. If starting and growing a business were easy, anybody could do it. Business is the most competitive, "real world" sport you'll ever find. And just like sports, the trophy goes to those who refuse to lose and find creative ways to win. That's why you should welcome the challenges of growing and expanding your business. It gets those competitive juices flowing and stirs your creativity, which helps you find new opportunities. It pumps me up to think of new and exciting ways to grow *Body By Jake*, Major League Lacrosse, and my other enterprises.

It's great when things are clicking, but there aren't many businesses that operate on cruise control. Most are dynamic, organic things that need to be nurtured just like you'd care for a big garden. You can't just plant the seeds and walk away, expecting it to thrive. Like a lot of entrepreneurs, I'm not a nuts-and-bolts, day-to-day-business kind of guy. I've hired some really great people to handle that so I can focus every day on finding new ways to grow our businesses and to provide more value to our customers.

| *Keep growing to keep going!*

Most businesses start small, including most of our nation's biggest corporations. Delta Air Lines began with one crop-dusting plane. Coca-Cola was first peddled as a medical elixir by an Atlanta pharmacist. A couple of brainy guys named Bill and Dave working in a garage started Hewlett-Packard. Their street-smart success should inspire you since all they had was $538 in start-up funds and a couple of screwdrivers. Their first product wasn't exactly a hit with the mass market either. How many people needed a resistance-capacitance audio oscillator? They called it the "HP Model 200A" because they thought it would make people think they'd been around awhile. Their first big sale was to a movie studio, which ordered eight of the oscillators to test recording equipment and speaker systems in a dozen movie theaters where they'd installed special sound systems. It was for the premiere of a strange new animated movie. The customer was Walt Disney. The movie was *Fantasia!*

| *Street smart entrepreneurs never quit!*

Don't you love history? Well, here's a reality check: History isn't exactly on your side when it comes to being a street-smart entrepreneur. The vast majority of new businesses fail—*unless*, you get smart about finding ways to keep them growing beyond the first few weeks, months, and years. So you've got to stay pumped about finding ways to help you grow your business! Being an entrepreneur doesn't end with starting a business, and I think that's great news!

Street-Smart Tips for Growing Your Business

1. DOUGH TO GROW

No, you aren't suffering from déjà vu. I did give you tips earlier on raising money, but that was just for the start-up period of your business. I hate to tell you this, but the need for cold cash keeps popping up at every stage of development, from start-up throughout the life of a business. It may sound scary, but even in down times it can be a good move to invest additional funds and prepare your business for growth over the long term. By preparing your business in the down times, you'll be ready to rip when the economy bounces back.

A recent study supports the old saying that it takes money to make money, according to a report in *Business Week*. The software giant Intuit did a survey of small business owners in 2004 and found that those who invest to help their businesses grow even in challenging times end up ahead of the game. Sixty-four percent of those who invested in their companies saw growth in the twelve months that followed, according to their survey. Their most common investments for growing their businesses were in advertising and marketing, new employees, new technology, and new products or services.

Business Week also reported that street-smart entrepreneurs who invested in accounting services were more likely to describe their company's growth as "significant." That's interesting to me because one of the things we did to spur growth at *Body By Jake* was to hire an experienced full-time chief financial officer. We've found that it really helps to have him on board and the survey bears that out. Nearly 62 percent of those polled said they looked to their accountants for new ways to cut overhead, while 49 percent said that their accountants helped them master new office technologies and improve performance.

| *Aim high. Then aim higher!*

When it comes to finding cash to grow your business, the good news is that often it's easier to get a loan from a bank or other financial institution once your business is up and running. That's particularly true if you've got a steady cash flow, a solid customer base, inventory, and other assets. As part of our preparations at *Body By Jake* Global LLC to ensure long-term growth, we set up a series of meetings with investment bankers and venture capital groups. Some of them were very professional and pleasant people to deal with, and it was interesting to talk with them. I just couldn't see giving any one else a piece of the company that I've worked so hard to build. After talking to nearly a dozen of them, I said the heck with it.

I'm sure there are some good venture capital groups out there, but I've got too much blood, sweat, and tears invested in my company to give any of it away. Maybe I'm just too much of a hard-core hard-headed entrepreneur, but it drives me nuts to think about giving someone a seat at the table just because they've got a pile of money to play with. Fortunately, we were in great shape financially. We were testing the waters. If we'd really needed a quick influx of cash, I probably would have found an investment group to work with.

Keep in mind that nothing is free in this world, especially money! Still, it was a great experience meeting with all of those money-minded people. It's interesting to see how they think and to hear their pitches. Some seemed like really sharp people, but my rule is that I don't want to do business with anyone unless it is someone I'd be willing to have over for dinner at the house. There's got to be chemistry and a lot of trust.

Unless you've got a degree in finance, it's easy to get baffled by fast-talking financiers. Remember that debt financing—getting a loan that you pay back with interest—is usually the least expensive way to borrow money for your business. Equity financing is a more costly way to do it because it involves giving up some of your equity or ownership in your own company, and I advise you to do that only after very careful evaluation of your future "partner."

| *Pick partners who are believers!*

Most lenders are wary of extending debt financing to businesses still in the early stages of development—the first six months to a year—because they want those loans repaid on a set schedule, plus interest of course. They also want to see enough collateral or assets to cover the full repayment price of the loan, which most businesses don't have in those early days. When you want to create a growth spurt for your business, you'll probably need well over $100,000 in cash. That kind of money usually comes with some serious strings attached if you are dealing with private investment firms or angel investors.

SBA Loans. If the thought of dealing with venture capitalists makes you want to go back to washing cars at the Suds N' Shine, don't worry. There are other options for finding dough to grow. The Small Business Administration can be a great resource for entrepreneurs. It offers a loan program called the "504" (not to be confused with Levi 504 jeans—although this loan program does have a "stretch fit" too). This program is designed to help small business expand. You can use the money to make big purchases, such as a property or a building, or major equipment and machinery. Most banks can help you apply for the SBA's 504. They'll explain that it's really two loans rolled into one, with the bank providing 50 percent, and another 40 percent coming from a nonprofit community development corporation (CDC). You'll have to ante up 10 percent, which is why they call this a 50-40-10 or 504 loan. One advantage of 504s is that small businesses can borrow up to $5 million, and sometimes even more. So it's worth checking out. True, you'll have to jump through some hoops and deal with government red tape, but Uncle Sam can be easier to deal with than the guys in shiny suits!

2. DEVELOP NEW PRODUCTS OR BRANDS

I encourage street-smart entrepreneurs to always be open to developing new product lines and new brands as a way of growing their businesses. To me, that's exciting stuff. Of course, I don't want you to do a deal just to do a deal. Make sure it's a good fit for your company, that it matches up with your interests, and that it adds to the appeal of your brand or your company. You can't be afraid to try new approaches for growing, but don't stretch yourself too thin or endanger the strength of your company by trying to do too much too fast.

We probably get at least thirty calls a day from individuals and companies that want to do business with *Body By Jake*. We listen to every pitch because even if we don't buy what they say, you never know when it might spark an idea for a new product or brand that will help us grow the company. We have a number of *Body By Jake*-branded and sub-branded fitness-related products, including the Ab Scissor, the Total Body Trainer, and Thermo Burn. Because my *Body By Jake* brand is widely known, we've got tremendous opportunities to grow our business by increasing the number of our branded exercise equipment products on the market and also to expand the brand's reach in other fitness-related enterprises, such as home fitness videos, food, apparel, and nutritional supplements.

| *Do the deals!*

Over the years, we've had a lot of companies approach us about licensing deals for *Body By Jake* sports wear and workout clothing. We've played around with the idea but I've never jumped in with both feet because I haven't found the right partner. As of this writing, however, we are in discussions with a sporting goods chain that wants to be our sole retail partner for our fitness products. We have not had a huge presence in retail with our fitness products outside of our infomercial products.

As of this writing, we are working on an exclusive branding deal with a chain that would become the only place you can get BBJ fitness products, ranging from weight benches to cardio equipment as well as infomercial items. It'll be a terrific deal if it works. This is a chain with more than 1000 stores and a very classy operation. We are helping each other build our brands because we hope it will drive more traffic into their stores.

I'm not the only entrepreneur or business owner to grow my business by producing new products under my brand, or creating whole new brands. Even the best-known brands are doing it, from Vanilla Coke to mint-flavored Tylenol Extra Strength Cool Caplets. The pain pill maker developed the mint-flavored brand to try and win a bigger share of the youth market and, according to *Fortune* magazine, it spent $2.5 million to fund events like skateboarding competitions, break dancing contests, and snowboarding exhibitions to promote it. One of the wildest efforts I've seen to create spin-off brands and spur growth is the new product introduced by the Krispy Kreme donut franchise. As a health-and-fitness role model I'm not much into downing donuts (I just eat the holes, which are unbelievably low in carbs!). But this new product really caught my eye. Who'd ever imagined Krispy Kreme soda?

| *The biggest risk is not taking one!*

For the last few years the Krispy Kreme company has experienced incredible growth and popularity as they expanded their franchise stores and also put Krispy Kreme kiosks in grocery and convention stores. When things began to slow down for them, they tried to spur growth by expanding their brand with Frozen Original Kreme—a donut you can drink. I'm not endorsing Krispy Kreme in either pastry or drinkable form, but I do think it's interesting that they are stepping out of the donut box and trying something a little risky and a lot different in order to keep growing. You've got to be willing to do that. Don't be foolhardy but don't be afraid either. Keep any new products or services within the umbrella of what you know and do best. And test the heck out of the market before you throw a lot of precious dollars at manufacturing and marketing. But be willing to try new and fresh approaches. You might be surprised at what works!

You've heard the expression "I've got a lot of irons in the fire," right? Well, that's an old cowboy term, meaning that there's a lot of branding to do back on the ranch. I want you to keep a lot of brands in the fire when it comes time to grow your business. It's a matter of keeping those entrepreneurial fires going every day. That's one of the things I like about my business. We're always introducing new products, so it's almost like starting a new company over and over again.

One of the best examples I can think of is Steve Jobs at Apple. Once he returned to the company that he created, Jobs brought it back from some very difficult times. He did it by cutting costs and simplifying product lines, but he also did it by re-creating Apple's image. He changed it from a company that made hip, smart, innovative, and well-designed computers and software, to one that makes all sorts of hip, smart, innovative, and well-designed products. He opened Apple up so that it now not only makes cutting-edge computers, it also is a leader in digital music, wireless base stations, and software for making movies and music. With entirely new products like the iPod, Jobs and Apple are broadening the company's demographic base to pave the wave for even more growth. According to *Business Week*:

There's evidence that the iPod, plus Apple's growing retail presence, is putting the Mac bug in the brain of a far broader demographic of potential customers—including women, kids, and others who are not typical PC buyers.

They call this a "halo" affect because the creation of one wildly popular new product, the iPod, has made all of the other Apple products more appealing to a broader market. That's another reason for you to be willing to consider new brands and new products as a way of growing your business too!

3. GROW ONLINE AND REACH NEW MARKETS

Back in the mid-1990s, the buzz for entrepreneurial businesses was that if you didn't have a Web site up and running for your customers, you were going to be left in the dust. It was like the Gold Rush all over again in California—in more ways than one. Companies with strong brands, like ours, were swamped with calls from venture capitalists and their geeks-for-hire. "The days of bricks and mortar businesses are over!" they claimed. "If you aren't doing business online, you'll be out of business in six months!"

They were all over us to nail down a BodyByJake.com domain name and launch a Web site so they could then take it public and reap millions in instant profits. It scared the bejesus out of me, to tell you the truth. Call me old-fashioned, but I happen to believe that you shouldn't sell stock in a company—even a dot-com company—until you have the profits to prove your viability in the marketplace. A lot of the companies that were being launched in those days were all flash and no cash. This Gold Rush, like the first one, ended in calamity for the vast majority of those who staked a claim without first testing to see if there was anything beneath the surface. Once again, I went with my gut and told the venture capitalists to take their dot-com dollars somewhere else.

We saw the Internet as a great way to grow our business, but we weren't about to give away the company store to get in the dot-com game. Instead, we did secure our domain name as BodyByJake.com, and then we built a Web site as carefully and as thoughtfully as we do everything else. We didn't try to make a quick score by going public and selling stock just in our Web-based business. We played for the long term gains by incorporating our Web-marketing with the rest of the company. And we're reaped incredible rewards since we first went online with our Web site in 1997.

Today, more than 20 percent of our sales are conducted online through our Web site, and that percentage is growing every month! Meanwhile, back at the dot-com Gold Rush, companies like DrKoop.com were seeing their values driven into the stratosphere by speculative investing. As *Fortune* magazine and others reported, the start-up dot-com bearing the brand of the former U.S. Surgeon General had taken in less than $ 1.5 million in revenues but investors went crazy for its stock. They drove up its market value to $1.3 billion before it deflated by more than 90 percent in less than a year. I'm sure some people—most likely the venture capitalists who got in and got out quickly—made a lot of money, while millions of investors lost billions in the dot-com crash.

Still, now that things are settling down, my business and many others have learned that doing business online can help fortify your brand and help your bricks and mortar business grow to new heights in some very exciting ways. While infomercials are still our bread and butter, the World Wide Web is definitely the land of opportunity for even greater growth. I'm sure that's no surprise there for the Web-heads out there, but you don't have to be a certified software engineer to jump into the online marketplace. That's the great thing about it. The Internet and e-commerce are accessible to small business owners and street-smart entrepreneurs who may not yet be able to afford more expensive methods for growing their businesses. You don't need hundred of thousands of dollars to open up an online store, and it doesn't matter that you don't know Java from Unix. Hey, the microwave in our kitchen is my idea of high-tech.

The good news is that there are plenty of Web wizards out there willing to help you build a Web site and pitch your products or services online for affordable rates. We'll get into a little of the technical stuff, but first let's look at some of the basics of e-commerce. E-okay?

E-Commerce 101. There's no doubt that the Internet is a great business tool that helps even small businesses compete with the big boys. It's just a great and highly efficient way to market and sell your products by reaching those who are looking for whatever you are selling. Forrester Research, Inc. estimates that 47.3 million North American homes have online access and 43.9 percent have someone who has browsed online. Of that 43.9 percent, 65 percent have made purchases! Those are the kinds of percentages that make street-smart entrepreneurs snap to attention!

| *The Internet levels the playing field!*

Because of big online marketers like Amazon.com, eBay, Travelocity.com, and scores of others, busy shoppers are increasingly comfortable with going online, finding what they want, and paying with their credit cards. That opens the door for street-smart entrepreneurs to go places with their businesses where they might never have gone before. Even if you have an esoteric business selling greasy old car parts for 1963 Chevy Novas, vintage clothes scavenged from old department stores, or hair pieces made from squirrel fur, the best place to find people looking for your products is on the World Wide Web! Once you have a Web site up and running, the wonders of the Web go to work for you. Someone only has to type a description of your product or service—or your brand name—into one of the search engines like Google or Yahoo, and *Voila!* you've got a new customer! (Does anybody really know what *Voila!* means?)

| *Be a "net-preneur!"*

If your product or service is something marketed to other businesses like accounting software or janitorial services, you should know that the Internet has become a major shopping place for business owners too. In recent years, business-to-business e-commerce has become a $1.5 trillion dollar market, according to Forrester Research. In fact, many of the biggest corporations now demand that their suppliers deal with them online. Federal contracts are also going online, so if your market includes government agencies you'll need to connect with them on the Net.

Any street-smart entrepreneur who wants to grow a business has got to be something of a "net-preneur." Whether your business is selling daisies, making music, or cleaning swimming pools, you need to understand that more and more people use the Internet as both their "yellow pages" and as their shopping mall. For small businesses especially, the Net levels the playing field, allowing even highly-specialized niche marketers to reach a World Wide Web of customers just like the big corporations. It's interesting to watch the Web because of that. The consumer marketplace is like one big jungle but thanks to e-commerce the big cats are no longer king.

Look at Amazon.com. It was launched as an online competitor to all of the huge bookstores that had become dominant around the country. They had to scramble to create their own online bookstores to compete because Amazon.com had some huge advantages. It didn't have to spend millions to build stores and staff them with employees. But something else happened too. The huge bookstore chains had made it tough on small independent bookstores to compete, but those that plugged into the Internet with their own Web sites soon found that they too could sell books online. Now many of them have linked to the Web sites of the Amazon.com so that shoppers can check out their shelves too. It's as if the jungle gerbils were hunting alongside the lions and tigers! (Okay, that's my last effort at being metaphorical, at least in this chapter.)

You've probably surfed the Web for music, books, or other items yourself. Most people have become accustomed to "Googling" or "Yahooing" for homework or business information and to "IM-ing" buddies to stay in touch, so you may know the basics. But if you aren't a real tech whiz, you probably don't have much of an idea of how it all works.

Believe it or not, the Internet began in the late 1960s as a military communications system. The idea was to create a bunch of interconnected networks instead of one centralized system so that it couldn't be easily knocked out by the bad guys, whoever they might be. To link all of the networks together, scientists developed the TCP/IP (Transmission Control Protocol/Internet Protocol). That's about as high-tech as I'm going to get with you. It's enough for you to know that it is what enables your computer in Kokomo to talk to your sister's computer in Katmandu. Once the Department of Defense got the ball rolling and made it possible for computer networks to hook up, geeks around the world began hooking up. They now rule the world! Or at least a good part of it. There are now more than 40 million people worldwide plugged into the World Wide Web and it's growing by millions every month.

Create Your Own Web Site. In the 1980s, it got a whole lot easier to create a network connection when the Webmasters got rid of numeric addresses for Web sites and allowed for the creation of domain names. That marked the beginning of the whole "dot-com" thing. It's a lot easier for people to track down your Web site if it's named JoJosGym.com instead of 359.32.909.

I'm not the guy to give you step-by-step advice for creating a Web site. It used to be that you had to hire a Web designer to do it but now there are a zillion (really, I counted them!) free places online that guide you through the process step by step. If you have no geek genes or if you tend to wear stripes with checks, it still might be worth it to hire a professional web designer who can give you a first class site. Remember your Web site will be the way hundreds or thousands or even more people learn about your business, so you want to do it right. And creating a Web site can get complicated fast if you plan on selling, billing, and shipping from it. You'll have to buy equipment and bring in some experts to help you unless you've got the gift yourself. To get an idea of what is involved, just go to your favorite search engine site like Google or Yahoo, type in "create a Web site," and see what pops up.

One thing I would advise you to do quickly: Register your Web site name as soon as you decide what you want it to be. It's really easy to do. Get online and go to either InterNIC (www.internic.com) or one of the name registration services such as www.register.com. There you can do a name search to make sure that the domain name you want to use hasn't been taken yet. If it's all clear, then you just complete the online registration form to stake your claim to the name. Or, you can select an Internet Service Provider (ISP) to host your Web site and the service provider will register your domain name with the Internet's Network Information Center.

| *Lure customers into your Web!*

You should be able to get an ISP to host your Web site for between $25 and $50 a month. There are also lots of free hosting services out there, but there are usually e-strings attached to the free hosting sites. (That's e-strings, not G-strings, please.) Most will want to put advertisements on your Web site, which can clutter things up like billboards along the highway. And your free host will want to track and monitor visitors to your Web site with cookies or other online software that many people see as invasions of their privacy because the hosts often sell information to marketing services. So, before you go that route, think about whether it might cause bad vibes with your customers or clients.

How does having a Web site help you grow your business? Well, for one thing, it's the hottest advertising and marketing medium out there. It's a whole lot cheaper and faster to have a Web site that people can find in the blink of an eye than to pay for commercials on television or radio or to buy ads in most newspapers. Once again, the Net helps your business compete with the big dogs. Let's say you are selling handmade fly-fishing lures or ponytail scrunchees (Can you tell I've got a daughter?). Once you've got a Web site that lists the names of your products, you don't have to hunt for customers. They can find you by typing "fly-fishing lures" or "scrunchees" into their favorite search engines.

Of course, you still have to find ways to stand out from all of the other lure- or scrunchee-makers out there because there's a whole lot of folks selling on the Web. So don't think you can just lie back and watch the orders roll in. Get creative. Stay aggressive. Watch what the competition is doing. And remember that the same "truth in advertising rules" apply online as everywhere else. You can't mislead people or make claims about your products or services that aren't true. Otherwise the Federal Trade Commission may come a-knockin' on your door. Even worse, unhappy customers will spread the word on the Web that your company doesn't play fair, and once that happens, you might as well shut down the Web site. The Internet levels the playing field in that way too!

Here is a list to help you when you are considering growing your business with a Web site:

- Will you need someone else to build your site or will you do it yourself?

- Will you need someone to custom program it for sales, billing and shipping?

- Who will host your site?

- How are you going to process credit card orders and how will they be transmitted to your merchant account?

- How will you get your order and fulfillment information into your accounting system?

- Are you going to farm out most of the technical stuff? If so, don't rush into hiring the first Web design firm you find. Before you sign on the dotted line, talk to at least four or five of them so that you get a good handle on the price range and the different service packages they offer.

> *E-mail is great but don't lose the personal touch. Pick up the phone!*

- Have you ever dashed off an e-mail that someone interpreted the wrong way? It happens a lot because people can't see your face or hear your voice. Keep that in mind as you set up your business Web site. It's a very handy and efficient way to do business but sometimes the personal touch gets lost in all the high-tech. Don't get overly reliant on e-mail. Often it is better to pick up the phone for important communications, but it is also important to make sure your site is user-friendly, and to follow up purchases with thank-you e-mails. Regular e-mail newsletters or sales announcements are also a way to keep the bonds strong with customers on the Web.

- This one is beyond old low-tech Jake, but the Web wizards at *Body By Jake* and Major League Lacrosse tell me that a lot of people who design their own business Web sites make a serious mistake that cuts them off from a whole lot of sales opportunities. They forget to use Meta or Title tags in their HTML codes that help search engines find them for potential customers browsing the Web. When you consider that e-commerce sites get as much as 50 percent of their business from Web searches, that's a big mistake to make! So don't you, or your hired geek, forget to do that!

▪ Make sure you test your Web site thoroughly before customers find it. Figure that anything that can go wrong, will go wrong, so check it out. If people visit your site and can't get what they want, or it screws up their orders, they'll go Google the competition. Don't let that happen! If you have to, hire a geek just to check your work. Do it!

▪ Once you've got your business Web site up and running, make sure you tell your customers about it. What's the sense of spending time and money on a street-smart site if you don't let your customers and potential customers know about it? We put our Web site address in all of our television and print material so that people can find us online. That's absolutely critical. You wouldn't open up a shop and just expect people to find you, would you? We've found that our online store works best when we aggressively promote it in our television and print spots. Our television infomercials drive our online business. So, make sure you put it on your business cards, stationery, and list the www.yourWebsitelocation.com in all of your advertising and marketing too—including the Yellow Pages and newspaper and television ads. You wouldn't leave off your telephone number or address would you? So, make sure you tell them where you live on the Web!

▪ Make sure you are ready for the rush if your Web site works wonders! When Bodybyjake.com first went online, we had so many orders come in it not only blew our servers, it knocked out the power grid for the entire West Coast!! Okay, maybe I exaggerated just a little (we did have a light bulb burn out in the supply room). We've been around long enough that we always have a pretty accurate read on how many sales will be generated by any and all of our tools, whether it is infomercials or the Internet. But there have been a lot of cases where street-smart net-preneurs fired up a new Web site and it attracted so many hits they nearly had their lights punched out.

Often, people spend too much time wondering what will happen if they fail and not nearly enough time planning for success! Don't let that happen to you! Along with testing all aspects of your Web site to make sure they work, make certain too that the rest of your operation can handle it if people go wild for your product or services. Draw up contingency plans that map out what you will do to respond to increases in demand. Make sure you can produce enough products or service to meet booming demand. And plan ahead in case you need to add bandwidth from your Web hosting service, or consider buying your own servers and high-speed connections, so that you don't lose business to an Internet highway traffic jam.

| *Plan for success!*

▪ Keep it up to date! All the work you put into your Web site will go to waste if potential customers come to it and find Easter eggs on sale in July. When you are marketing in a mile-a-minute medium, your content needs to keep pace. Keep both the information and the design fresh so surfers will keep coming back. And keep your audience or market in mind. If you are selling products or services to the over-35 market, you don't want them to open a Web site that immediately plays "Rage Against the Machine" on their home computers! Understand who your online customers are and make your Web site user-friendly for them.

We work very hard to make sure that people enjoy the experience of visiting our Web site and purchasing products online. A Web site is different from a television show or even an infomercial in that people will always come back to television spots while flipping channels. But if they visit a Web site once and find it confusing, out of date, or difficult to navigate, they very likely won't come back.

| *Build a Web site that keeps 'em coming back!*

Get a Boost on eBay. Even if you have a bricks and mortar business, and a Web site too, you might also consider marketing your products or services on the world's biggest online flea market and auction house. Could nearly 500,000 other entrepreneurs be wrong? Wouldn't you like to tap into a market that has nearly $15 billion in annual sales on 28 sites worldwide? Well, eBay is the place where all of those street-smart entrepreneurs are tapping that huge market, and it is still growing dramatically by the click of a million mouses . . . err, mice.

I'd like to join about 2 billion other people right now in confessing that I wish I'd thought of this brilliant e-commerce concept. EBay can be a practical, absolutely brilliant way to bring together buyers and sellers. I don't think you can go wrong incorporating eBay into your business if your product or services fit its vast model—and if you take the time to learn how to do it right. EBay has proven to be an especially great place to sell books, DVDs, hot tickets to special events, real estate, collectibles, computer software and hardware, new clothing, home and garden supplies, industrial equipment, and business supplies. It really is a living, breathing example of the global marketplace in action. And man, is there a lot of action. It's one of the fastest ways imaginable to move product if you've got product to move.

In some ways, it's even better than creating your own Web store because there are so many people shopping on eBay you just get hundreds and even thousands of "hits" a day. *Entrepreneur* magazine reported the eBay tale of Jesse Nyman, president of Nyman's Jewelry Inc. in Fort Myers, Florida. When he started using eBay about six years ago, he sold $300 in jewelry even though he now admits the photographs he used weren't exactly top quality. After that success, he began doing a lot more business on eBay. Even though he has a Web site too, Nyman says 70 percent of the $1 million he made in sales in 2003 was done on eBay. The giant auction house has proven especially effective in attracting overseas jewelry suppliers to his business, he told the magazine.

I love the simplicity of the eBay model. Heck, I just love going to their site and seeing what kind of wild stuff they've got out there. Where else can you get 15,640 Elvis items in one place? (There really were that many when I tried it!) As a street-smart "net-preneur," you can post your items for sale in an auction that goes on for up to ten days, or as a "buy it now" offering. But don't let the simplicity of eBay's business model lull you into jumping in before you've given careful study on how to make it work best—and safest— for your business. While it's relatively easy to get started, things can get complicated fast. EBay experts advise novices to consider that selling items in the global marketplace raises sometimes complex issues of licensing, pricing, shipping, and cultural questions.

You really should check out eBay just to see how it might work for you and your business, but do your homework. The eBay Web site offers step by step procedures for getting started. For more in-depth training, eBay University sity courses are offered around the country. The one-day sessions cost about $40. They offer both a basic and more advanced course. The basic course offers tips on selling, including how to create listings that bring in bidders and buyers. It also covers online payments with PayPal, monitoring listings, and transaction completion. The advanced "Beyond the Basics" course offers more selling, bulk-selling, and merchandising tips to grow your business on eBay. The material includes guidance on managing auctions and running an online eBay business efficiently.

As with your own Web site, you want to treat eBay customers right because if you don't, they can fire back at you with the site's feedback ratings system, which lets customers rate the sellers or "trading partners." Positive ratings from customers will increase your performance rating but negative rants about your lack of first-class service can drag your company name into the e-mud, where you may find it difficult to do business.

| Treat your eBay customers right.

Because you have to pay the folks at eBay a percentage for using their Web site, you should be very careful about how you price your products or services. Don't give away the company store just so you can be an eBay merchant too. Market value rules pricing on eBay. Smart shoppers surf for the best prices, so competition can be intense, and your profit margins can be eaten alive by the fees you pay eBay for space on its site. EBay experts advise that selling your products in this global marketplace can be very rewarding but there are many skilled players in this game. You can't just sit back and watch. To do it right, you have to be creative in designing your "stall" in the marketplace, and you've got to monitor it carefully.

4. GROW WITH GOVERNMENT CONTRACTS

If your street-smart business offers products or services that can be marketed and sold to the military, NASA, or any other government agency or department, then you shouldn't let fear of red tape or bureaucratic bologna scare you off. If I could figure out a way to get the Pentagon to be a *Body By Jake* customer, believe me, I'd do it.

Come to think of it, I think the White House could use an Ab Scissor in the Oval Office, don't you? How about the Lincoln bedroom?

Doing business with Uncle Sam can open red, white, blue, and golden opportunities, if you are willing to put in the time and effort to learn how government bidding and contracts work. It's true also that because the government tends to tie smaller contracts together in large bundles, it can be difficult for small businesses to compete with bigger companies in securing deals. It can also be a giant pain in the buttissimo to register, apply for contracts, and deal with the bureaucracy. I'm not going to sugar-coat that it takes a lot of time and hard work to negotiate the maze and to figure out how to sell to government agencies and departments. But if you have a product or service they need, Uncle Sam can be a great guy to do business with.

Government agencies and departments generally have "procurement processes" that business owners have to endure—I mean, follow—to compete for contracts. There are basic steps to the process, which are similar to those followed by most big corporations.

Here are the usual steps:

▪ Contact the department's procurement officer and ask whether there are any contracts that your business might apply for. If you qualify as a minority business owner, there might be some set-asides for businesses like yours.

▪ If your business has the products or services they're looking for, you'll be given an information packet with forms to fill out. It'll ask for references, financial records, and a history of any other government contracts you've had. Fill out the forms and return them. If yours is a minority-owned firm, you will probably need to get certified by the National Minority Supplier Development Council or a similar organization in your region.

▪ You may be told to contact buyers within the agency or department and, if all goes well, your company could be entered into a database that government buyers across the county can access.

▪ Don't sit around and wait for them to call you. Market your business by staying in touch with any government buyers you can contact. Build a relationship with your contacts and understand that it can take years to get in the door, but once you've proven that you are a reliable supplier, it can be very lucrative.

| *Uncle Sam is an uncle you can bank on.*

In the last few years, the federal government has streamlined the process for getting government contracts for small businesses. Naturally, they gave it a bureaucratic-sounding name to baffle everyone. It's called the Integrated Acquisition Environment (IAE) and it is administered by the General Services Administration (GSA). This program helps small businesses deal with the process of getting government contracts by simplifying procedures—in part by putting a lot of them online for easier access.

The Small Business Administration (SBA), which can be the street-smart entrepreneur's best friend in government, now offers a "business matchmaking program" that hooks up companies with the right people in government agencies that have contracts to award. The SBA also has workshops around the country that teach small business owners how to get government contracts. Those workshops are worth checking out because you are likely to make valuable contacts within the bureaucracy. Hey, they may be boring bureaucrats, but they've got a big pot of money to spend. Think of it as a way of getting some of your tax dollars back—and maybe a whole lot more.

To learn more about federal contracts and how you can tap into the government procurement system, check out the Web site of the Small Business Administration (www.sba.gov) and also its business matchmaking program, done in association with Hewlett Packard at www.businessmatchmaking.com.

5. PARTNER UP FOR MUTUAL GROWTH

Earlier in the chapter, I told you that *Body By Jake* was looking at teaming up with a sporting goods chain to expand our brand into the retail market. That sort of partnership is sometimes known as a "strategic alliance," which sounds like a good name for the next Star Wars sequel to me, but I like the concept. Teaming up with another business that complements yours is another great way to grow as long as you are careful in how you structure the deal. You've also got to make sure the two companies are compatible. One of my very unscientific measures is whether I'd want to spend the weekend hanging out with the top executives. If they are street-smart and straightforward people who do business in an ethical way, then I'm usually okay with partnering up with their company.

Strategic alliances only work if both businesses benefit from the deal. You can't go into them being selfish or trying to take more than you give. You may get away with that once, but the other company will never deal with you again—and word will get around that you aren't a good person to deal with. You don't want that to happen. I've said it before and I'll say it again, it's all about relationships. And my latest strategic alliance for Major League Lacrosse is a great example of that. It also offers proof that one good strategic alliance can lead to another.

| *Both sides have to benefit to make it work!*

Body By Jake has had great success partnering with the Home Shopping Network over the years. They've helped us connect to thousands and thousands of customers and we're one of their best-selling clients. One of the good people I met at HSN was its company president and chief operating officer, David Dyer, who left there to become the head guy at Lands' End a couple years ago. He'd worked at Lands' End previously and they thought so much of him they brought him back to lead the company out of a downturn, which he did, interestingly enough by cutting a deal for Sears to buy Lands' End. It was regarded as a very smart move. David got Lands' End right-side up within a year, and shortly after that, he got another job offer. Clothing designer and manufacturer Tommy Hilfiger asked him to become CEO of his global corporation in 2003.

Being a patient and cautious street-smart kind of guy, I gave David about an hour and a half to settle into his new job at Tommy Hilfiger Corp. Then I called him and asked if I could meet Tommy and pitch him on a strategic alliance with Major League Lacrosse. The game had come a long way since Native Americans first started playing it on the prairies. But the wardrobe was out of whack! We had the fastest game on two feet with the slowest looking uniforms. The league needed a serious fashion makeover, and I felt Tommy was the guy to do it!

So I called David, his new CEO. And my buddy responded just like I thought he would.

"Jake, I just got here!" he said.

"Hey, I'm trying to help you make a name for yourself so you can impress the big boss," I told him.

I told David that I thought Major League Lacrosse needed a style makeover and, since it's the hottest sport in the universe, maybe Tommy would want to get in the game with us. Brilliant guy that he is, David agreed.

In my crusade to make lacrosse the major league sport it deserves to be, I've formed partnerships with major American brands like Anheuser-Bush, New Balance, Gatorade, and, now, Tommy Hilfiger. David set up the meeting for me with the designer, who had created a very successful global company after his first entrepreneurial effort—a clothing store in his hometown of Elmira, New York—had gone bankrupt because it was too cutting edge. (Remember that: Don't Quit!!!)

Tommy is a very cool, laid-back guy. When we first met at his offices in New York City to talk about the prospect of forming a strategic alliance, he was casually dressed—for him—in a blazer, dungarees, and tennis shoes. I'd prepared a big pitch because I feared Tommy might not buy into the idea of designing sports uniforms. I wanted to sell him on the fact that lacrosse is the nation's hottest sport among the young "extreme" sports crowd that sets fashion trends for their generation. Even in my neighborhood in Pacific Palisades, groups of kids walk around the downtown shops in lacrosse gear, carrying their sticks, and looking cool. (Is cool still cool?)

So, I had all this material together to tell Tommy about the benefits his company might derive from hooking up with Major League Lacrosse, but just as I was beginning my rap-a-doo, he interrupted me in mid-sentence. Then a very strange thing occurred. I realized that Tommy Hilfiger was pitching me! I gotta confess, I loved it! It was one of those terrific moments of entrepreneurial Zen that occur when you plug into an opportunity that's so perfect it seems to be written in the cosmos!

He told me that in 1992, one of his designers came into his office with a

New York Rangers jersey, but he'd replaced the Rangers' logo with a Tommy Hilfiger emblem on the chest.

"What is this?" Tommy asked.

"It's going to be your hottest new line of clothing, and we're going to retail it for $148," the designer said.

Tommy couldn't believe that anyone would want to own a NHL hockey jersey with his name on it. He told the designer he didn't think it would work, but encouraged him to test the market anyway.

So, the designer—someone who didn't quit easy—did a little "guerilla marketing." They put the Tommy hockey jersey on a mannequin on the sales floor in Bloomingdale's Department Store in New York City. They wanted to see if any shoppers would notice it. Within a couple hours, they got a call from the Bloomingdale's buyer who said, "Send more!" It turned out that the Tommy hockey jerseys were a huge hit with hip hop artists like Snoop Dog and other musicians. They wore them around town and pretty soon, young people around the country were clamoring for them. Tommy told me that his line of hockey jerseys led to . . . are you ready for this? A billion dollar business!!

He told me that the hockey-jersey trend was beginning to level off so he was looking to make his mark in another sport. I darned near cried when he said:

"Jake, I'm really glad you are here because the timing is perfect. I think lacrosse is the next big thing."

Wow! I was floored! In fact, much to my delight, Tommy agreed to become one of the major sponsors for the league, and now we've got all kinds of great plans for increasing our strategic alliance! And we did it all on a handshake. He was as excited as me! He said they'd design a whole line of lacrosse wear and then promote them with some of the biggest, hippest music and movie stars! I love it!

You know, it's been a challenge creating a major sports league from scratch, but as a start-up, we have the flexibility to make deals and strategic alliances in a heartbeat. The older, more established leagues would take months to make a decision to even consider that kind of arrangement because they'd have to get all of the owners on board. Since my partners and I own the league, we can turn a deal on a dime and give you five cents change!

Strategic alliances are a big tool for growth, whether you're talking about a Fortune 500 company or a $500 dollar start-up. They can help your street-smart business get better market penetration, improve your product development, reduce costs, and create a hothouse where one opportunity creates another and another. As you can tell, I'm really enthusiastic about this growth pill for street-smart entrepreneurs, but I want you to read the warning on the label very carefully before you swallow. So here are my rules:

Jake's Rules for Street-Smart Strategic Alliances

- *Rule No. 1*: Make sure that each partner fully understands what the other partner wants to contribute to—and get out of—the deal, and that neither party signs on the dotted line until everyone is satisfied that they'll get what they want.

- *Rule No. 2*: Know who you are dealing with and know your partner's issues, challenges, and financial status before you draw up the terms of the strategic alliance.

- *Rule No. 3*: Get your own legal eagle of a lawyer to review the deal before you sign it.

- *Rule No. 4*: Make certain that your contract clearly defines prospective problem areas, such as ownership, licensing, manufacturing, and distribution rights. Make certain that it says who owns the rights to any technology, products, or applications that are created through the alliance.

- *Rule No. 5*: Make certain the contract for the alliance has language that defines when, how, and why it will be terminated and whether some licensing, production, or distribution rights may continue beyond the life of the alliance itself.

- *Rule No. 6*: You are the boss of the company, but your strategic alliance will affect everyone who works for you. So make certain that they are all on board—or that you know why they don't like the idea—before you sign the contract. Otherwise, they might make your life miserable, or spoil the deal for you later.

▪ *Rule No. 7*: Don't let a bigger company take advantage of you. If you are the smaller business in the alliance, don't get bullied, and don't get greedy. Either one will get you in trouble. Bigger companies may try to use their strength to get you to sign a bad agreement that benefits them more than it does you. They may claim that their influence and contacts are like money in the bank. Don't let them reap all the rewards for your creativity, hard work, and up-front risk. Stand your ground and they will respect you for it. If they don't, you wouldn't want to do business with them anyway!

Make no mistake, I really love strategic alliances as a method for growing businesses, but partnering up in business is like partnering up in romance. You've got to make sure you really know who you are dealing with. Even before you follow the rules I've given you, ask yourself these questions:

▪ What are some of the potential problems of this partnership—for either one of the parties involved?

▪ Is the timing right?

▪ Is there mutual respect between their top people and mine?

▪ Have we left ourselves room to grow, to maneuver, to get out of it if it doesn't work?

▪ Is there a process for settling disagreements that doesn't involve spending a fortune on lawyers?

▪ Have we laid out exactly who is responsible for what?

▪ Is this a win-win? (If it's not, get the heck out of there!)

▪ What does my lawyer think?

▪ What does my accountant think?

▪ What do my smartest advisors, employees, suppliers, and customers think?

▪ What does your own gut tell you?

That last one is critical to your survival as an entrepreneur. I've seen a lot of supposedly street-smart people go down the tubes because they stopped trusting the very instincts that made them successful in the first place. This is going to sound like one of Yogi Berra's classic lines, like "Nobody goes there anymore, it's too crowded!" But the truth is that the key to being a successful street-smart entrepreneur is to never stop being a street-smart entrepreneur. In other words, you should always keep that edge, that alertness, that awareness, and that faith in your own gut instincts that drove and directed you from the beginning! You've got to keep going and growing, and the best way to do that is to know the marketplace, read the trades, and listen to your employees and advisors. In the end, go with your gut and trust your heart!

risky business or frisky business?

SINCE I FOUNDED Major League Lacrosse, I've been finding myself in the company of a whole new group of street-smart entrepreneurs. I'm now meeting regularly with other professional sports team owners and league officials from the NFL and Major League Soccer. I also get invited to some pretty interesting affairs, at least for a kid who grew up in Baldwin, New York.

Not long ago, I was invited to a dinner banquet for entrepreneurs and business leaders in Omaha, Nebraska, of all places. We were flown there to hear words of wisdom from the "Oracle of Omaha," the billionaire investor Warren Buffett. His publicly-traded holding company, Berkshire Hathaway, owns a wide range of companies, including GEICO Insurance, Fruit of the Loom, Pampered Chef, and See's Candies, as well as major shares in big name brands like Coca-Cola.

I've always heard that Omaha is lovely in the spring, so I accepted the invitation from one of Buffett's companies that I do business with. Who'd pass up an opportunity to spend time with a guy reputed to be one of the smartest investors in America? The other people on our plane were no slouches. Most were very successful business entrepreneurs, and I'm here to tell you—thank my lucky stars—that they weren't really thrilled with the risky nature of this trip. We flew into a bunch of tornadoes and had to make an emergency landing on the way to the event. Then, on the way home, our plane had mechanical problems and did a sudden dive that had all of us doing the white knuckle thing. We fell 5,000 feet so fast that the oxygen masks dropped out of the overhead compartments!

You hear a lot of talk about entrepreneurs being risk-takers and thrill-seekers. But the hot-shot entrepreneurs on that plane wanted nothing to do with the risks we dealt with on those two flights! They'd much rather work every angle to make certain the odds are in their favor. Me too!

That's why I've always been reluctant to use the R-word when talking about entrepreneurship. There are so many stereotypes and misconceptions out there about the relationship between the two. Often, entrepreneurs are portrayed as impetuous, devil-may-care, thrill-seeking risk-junkies. It's very sexy stuff, I know, and it kind of tickles me. Risk? Getting on an airplane and flying into nine tornados is plenty risky for me. Besides, I live in Los Angeles. I drive to work everyday. That makes me a risk-taker before I even reach the office! Throw in the occasional earthquake and the threat of being run down by a mob of paparazzi chasing some starlet, and I'm probably over the top when it comes to living a high-risk life! But when it comes to business, I prefer to keep risk to a bare minimum—and so do most other street-smart entrepreneurs.

It's true that my personality naturally tends toward taking risks. But that's why I surround myself with people who aren't afraid to say, "No!" Instinctively, I'm more the guy who takes the flying leap than the one who spends his life wondering what's on the other side. But I am not a foolhardy risk-taker when it comes to business. Think about smart risk-taking versus foolhardy risk-taking this way: When you go to a swimming pool for the first time, you naturally want to test the water temperature. Well, the smart risk-takers dip one foot in. Foolhardy risk takers jump in with both feet!

Death-defying entrepreneurial Evel Knievels are few and far between. Most of us are very good at finding ways to reduce risks. Street-smart entrepreneurs are like Hollywood stunt professionals. Naturally, people think of them as daredevils because they are always diving off buildings or falling off horses. But that's just the illusion created for film. A few of them may be risk-takers, but most stunt professionals I've known are meticulous, careful people who are very much interested in living through each stunt so that they can die another day, on camera.

Stunt professionals and most street-smart entrepreneurs are experts at reducing risk to minimal levels before they make a leap. They measure the distance over the canyon. They strap on parachute or bungee cords. They set up two-story foam rubber cushions down below. And they may even push a dummy over the edge first just to test wind direction! That's why I prefer to say that my kind of entrepreneurs practice frisky business rather than risky business! We are daring but not dopey. We push the limits but we know where the boundaries are. We strive but we survive! We do not, I repeat, do not jeopardize all that we've built, all that we've attained, or the welfare of those we care about, just for the sake of a cheap thrill or a quick big score. Get it? Got it? Good!

| *Reduce the risk, then take the leap!*

This is important stuff because taking risks is a very necessary part of being an entrepreneur and growing your business. But you have to look before you leap, get the facts, and check your gut. To a casual observer, it may sometimes look like an entrepreneur is risking it all, but it's sort of like those movie shots of the guy diving off the top of a building or jumping a motorcycle over the flaming cars—you can't see all of the preparation and planning and safety nets that went down before the cameras were rolling!

Never Jump Without a Net

From the very moment that I began to talk about starting Major League Lacrosse, the whispers started. Actually, they were more like screams:

Sounds awful risky, Jake!

Are you sure you want to try such a high-risk deal?

Why would you take on that kind of risk?

Hey, I knew it wasn't going to be a stroll down Park Avenue. Starting a professional sports league from scratch was the most challenging thing I've ever done as a businessman. But there were still many ways to reduce the risk to manageable levels. I understand that you probably aren't looking to launch your own professional sports league, but to give you an idea of how street-smart risk reduction works at any level, let's take a quick look at a few things that worked for me. They can help you make your venture more frisky and less risky.

1. PROTECTING YOUR ASSETS

There are levels of risk in any start-up, but the odds are that your first business venture won't be a high-risk deal. Still, whether it's your first business or your twenty-first business, you should always make certain that you do not put at risk either your core assets like your home or retirement savings, or your family's welfare.

| *Guard the nest egg.*

Believe me, those were major concerns when I decided to create Major League Lacrosse, the most high risk venture of my entrepreneurial career. I also took pains to totally separate this new venture from *Body By Jake* Global LLC. The street-smart entrepreneur doesn't jeopardize successful existing businesses, his partners in them, or their profits with new, higher risk ventures. It's not like ripping off parts of one old car to rebuild another. The idea is to build two successful companies, not to tear apart one to build the other!

2. PARTNERING UP

A common way to reduce risk in a new venture is to spread it around so that instead of one person facing high levels of risk, you have several people dealing with manageable levels of it. If you bring in the right people there should be no problem sharing both the risk and the reward. You've got to make sure that your partners, shareholders or investors are people you want to do business with day in and day out. And you have to clearly define everyone's role, management responsibilities and exit plan in legal contracts.

As I've already told you, my partners in Major League Lacrosse are David Morrow, the founder of Warrior Lacrosse, and Tim Robertson, my friend and longtime business associate from my days with the Family Channel. They both bring a lot to the party. Tim is a financial professional with a wealth of experience in the media and entertainment industries. David, of course, knows this sport inside and out as a legendary player and as an entrepreneur who built his highly successful business around it. Having these two savvy guys on board probably cut my risk by two-thirds, at least!

3. CREATING MULTIPLE REVENUE STREAMS

What is risk, really? In business, when you talk about risk, it mostly boils down to assets and debits. To keep it going over the long term, you've simply got to have more money coming in than you are paying out. Sure, there are ways to run a business in the red and still keep it going because of tax benefits and other intricate financial dealings, but for our purposes let's keep it simple: Any business that I start, or that you start, has to make a profit over the long term to stay alive.

I know what you are thinking! And the answer is that as of this writing, Major League Lacrosse is not turning a cash profit—yet! Honestly, we've pumped a lot of money into it. That's something we expected. We knew it was going to take regular infusions of cash to bring this baby to life. The good new is that overall, the league is increasing in value every day, which at this stage is even more important. Every day the league is alive, we get a little bit stronger.

| *Think long term.*

The price of ownership in an MLL team has risen dramatically because of all the work we've put into building a first-class operation with great facilities, top notch owners, major corporate sponsors and partners, and a television deal that assures coverage will grow as our fan base increases.

It's been a real challenge putting the MLL together and nursing it through the first few years. Now we're looking at expanding with six more teams in the western United States by 2008, which offers a whole new set of challenges. And you know what? I love it! What true blue entrepreneur wouldn't? There are so many opportunities it's mind boggling! For someone who loves envisioning and putting together deals, this is the ultimate playground!

| *Build value and build a great life too!*

There are so many opportunities to create sources of revenue with a sports league. Ticket sales are just one aspect of it. Day in and day out, I'm making deals with corporate partners, sponsors, team owners, advertisers, it just goes on and on! I'm really thrilled that I've been able to get some of the greatest brand names in the world to join us as corporate partners and sponsors, including Anheuser-Busch, New Balance, Warrior Lacrosse, Gatorade, Tommy Hilfiger, Sporting News, Cascade, Sony Pictures, Paramount, Great Atlantic Lacrosse Company, and ESPN. Each and every one of them brings increased value that will only add to the strength of the MLL over the many years to come. And there's nothing better for reducing risk than long-term success! That's something that I've learned over the years with my first real business. Risks get easier to take when you've proven that your business has staying power!

Body By Jake **Makeover**

Four years ago, we made a move at *Body By Jake* that many people probably considered to be very high-risk. We did it to take our business to a higher level; it worked beyond our wildest dreams, but there were certainly no guarantees it would work out. We virtually reinvented the company. We went from being a business that just licensed our brand to other companies that took all the risks and reaped most of the profits, to being a company that takes the risks and reaps the rewards in far greater abundance.

This is not a move made in desperation, by any means. Sometimes, it takes hard times to push companies into taking risks, but I believe it's far better to operate from a position of strength than one of weakness. We were a small, strong company when we made our move to grow big. We did it by restructuring our approach. We had always been essentially just a brand-licensing company. We made our money from royalties—and we did very well. But we've gone gangbusters since we became a full-service fitness and media company. Over the years we had four different infomercial production companies as partners and we had done blockbuster infomercials with each and every one of them. But one by one, they hit rocky times because their other infomercial projects weren't as successful as ours. We finally decided that we knew enough about the infomercial business to run our own shows.

> *If you want to call all the shots, you've got to take the risks.*

We still hire out the expert help to produce the shows, but now we put up the money and reap the full rewards. We also handle our own "fulfill-ment," which means we collect the checks and credit-card payments and oversee distribution of our products. Before the change in our approach, we had a low-risk, low-overhead business with a high profit margin because we had no investment in capital products. But we weren't in control of our own destiny. Other people got to decide when they thought our products had peaked, when they should trigger retail sales, and when they should end a product's run.

That always bothered me. My name is on these products, and I wanted more control. So, I had to accept more risk, which really isn't so bad when you know what you are doing. We had watched and learned so much over the years that we were ready to step up and take control. We had become very protective of our brand's reputation, which made it hard for us to sit back and watch other people make key decisions. Even before we took charge, we were increasingly involved in all aspects of developing products, creating the marketing strategy, and doing much of the infomercial produc-tion even though we'd hired others to do that for us. The downside was that there weren't a lot of opportunities for us to grow in a big way—and you know me, go big or stay home!

We were coming off a very successful run with our *Body By Jake* Bun & Thigh Rocker. We were feeling very secure and confident. What a great time to shake things up. We had a good low-risk model, no bank debt, and no obligations. Yet, I felt that we weren't in control of our own destiny because we outsourced everything from manufacturing to buying media time, producing infomercials, and distributing our products. We weren't calling all the shots. And we had missed some financial opportunities.

We knew there were greater rewards out there if we were willing to take on more risk. And that is what led to our decision to take a leap and reinvent our company—the desire to achieve far greater growth than we could have created in any other way. We knew there was a big element of risk, but we did everything we could to trim it down. It wasn't really like starting over because we'd been in the business for fifteen years at that point. We knew where all the buttons, pulleys, and switches were. We'd just never punched or pulled them ourselves. We also felt that if we came across something that we didn't know how to do, we likely would know where to go for help.

All in all, the transition from licensing company to a more self-sufficient company went very smoothly and it has really increased the value of our business. Instead of recognizing a few million dollars in product royalties, we generated over $80 million in direct product sales in 2004. And because we hire entrepreneurial types and encourage them to be all they can be, we did it while only adding nine additional people to our staff!

Were there risks involved? Certainly! We could have stumbled out of the blocks if the first product we introduced turned out to be a turkey, but, of course, we made sure that it wasn't.

In fact, the first product out of the blocks for the reorganized *Body By Jake* Global LLC was the Total Body Trainer. It was a hit and we followed that up with our Ab Scissor, which turned out to be the biggest success in the history of our company! And our most recent product launch, the Cardio Cruiser, looks like it is going to be every bit as big—or even bigger—than the Ab Scissor.

We might have also run into problems if we hadn't been very careful when taking on complex tasks that we had previously outsourced, such as overseeing and dealing with hundreds of thousands of individual transactions, product returns, bad credit card charges, and other money matters. If our spreadsheets had been wrong, or if the fulfillment center wasn't processing returns properly, or if the customer service department failed to truly service our customers . . . well, the what-ifs are endless. But none of that happened because we did everything we could to manage and minimize risk.

It's interesting that one of the steps we took to reduce our risk while transitioning the company was to bring in greater financial expertise. In hindsight, our decision to change the way we did business looks like a brilliant move, but it took guts. It really was a major, life-altering change for *Body By Jake* Global LLC and for me too!

No Pain, No Gain

I learned as a bodybuilder that you can't build muscle or grow stronger simply by lifting the same amount of weight in every workout everyday. You've got to keep pushing yourself to new levels to stretch those muscle fibers and strengthen them. That's where they get the saying, "No pain, no gain." It's not that you have to actually hurt yourself or do damage, but you do have to get outside your comfort zone and push beyond the limits where you felt safe and secure. That's what life is all about!

Getting back to the bodybuilding stuff, risk management in the weight room consists of having someone "spot" you when you bench press so that you don't get hurt. In business, you manage risk with careful planning and expert support. But you also have to go with your gut. If you don't trust your own judgment and instincts, you probably don't belong in the game.

| *Street smart risk takers reduce risk to the minimum.*

Look at taking risks as part of the entrepreneurial life—with the caveat that you are responsible for managing risk to protect the long-term health of your business and the security of those you care about.

So far, the benefit has been tremendous for my companies. Our return on investment has multiplied enormously what it was because we were ready, willing and able to take a huge, but well-considered risk.

How do you manage risk in a street-smart way? Here are some tips:

1. DO A GUT CHECK FIRST!

Before we made the frisky decision to do the extreme Jake-over at *Body By Jake*, I checked my gut. I asked myself: *Is this move going to take you where you ultimately want to go?* Does the thought of where this takes the company really excite me because it fits my plan for my life? It's like going on the

Internet and using Mapquest.com when you are planning a trip. You get a map of where you want to end up, then you plug in where you are now, and finally, you click the button to decide how to get there.

| *Check your gut!*

Checking your gut involves tapping your imagination. Go somewhere quiet and think it through by playing out the scenarios in your mind. Where will this move take you over the next month, three months, six months, year, five years, and ten years?

It might help to write it down. Make two columns: one for the benefits or rewards that you might expect, the other for the possible downside. Hint: If the downside column is longer than the upside, check and double check to make certain that you've done all that you can to reduce the risk. If you've done that and the downside column is still longer than the upside column, it's time for a serious gut check to make certain that this is what you really want to do. Take your time. Listen to all of the wise people you can. But pay the most attention to what your heart tells you!

Before I decide to take a risk, I make a list showing all of the possible benefits and all of the potential challenges. I'm one of the most optimistic people you'll ever meet, so I sometimes have trouble even thinking of challenges. To compensate for my optimism, I'll call up friends who are more pragmatic and see what they come up with in terms of the downside. Then, I play out the scenarios in my head. I envision myself making the decision to make the leap and then I go through the same process as if I'd decided to walk away. I try to foresee all possible outcomes so that, when I actually make the decision, there aren't a lot of surprises.

So, even when the negative side is longer after you've written it down, if your instincts say to go with it, I believe you've got to give it a roll. Walk carefully! Put the flashlights on! But go with your gut!

2. DON'T BE AFRAID TO PULL THE PLUG

I know I've told you that my natural disposition is usually to get frisky and go for it, but I'm not afraid to yank the plug after thinking things through carefully—even when it's very tempting to make the leap. Several years ago,

I was really tempted to jump into the celebrity restaurant craze with a bunch of other health and fitness folks. This was back when Planet Hollywood, the House of Blues, and the Hard Rock Cafe were going strong so everyone—from supermodels to Harley-Davidson bikers—was jumping on the trend. A few of my friends were investors in those places and they suggested that a restaurant chain that promoted healthy eating might find a ready market. I liked the idea, so I set up a meeting at the Hotel Bel-Air in Los Angeles with other brand name fitness fanatics, including Kathy Smith, Tamilee Webb, Jack LaLanne, and Richard Simmons. Jane Fonda was interested but politely declined because of other commitments, especially her recent marriage to Ted Turner.

It was the first time we'd all gotten together, and it was a great moment and a fun experience. And it was a real soup-and-salad fest. Everybody agreed that the time was ripe for a restaurant catering to people who wanted to eat out without piling on the calories. We thought the theme for a guilt-free restaurant with healthy foods should be "heaven on earth," and so we named our restaurant *Eden*. I still think it was a great concept. It wasn't going to be just rabbit food like wheat grass and sprouts. We were going to have hamburgers made of lean beef, cheeseburgers with low-fat cheese, roasted rather than fried chicken, and even low-cal pizzas. I told everyone that I allowed myself to have desserts on Saturdays only, so they decided to call our entire menu "Every day is Saturday!"

We had a lot of fun cooking up ideas and menu items during the early planning stages. The Hamburger Buns of Steel was a natural, of course, as were the special lean Buttissimo Steak, the Don't Quit Quiche, and the Roast Thighs to Die For. (Okay, I made those up just for you.) Once I had partners lined up and psyched up, I began meeting with professional restaurant consultants to select a team to manage the restaurant chain for us. I also tried to get suggestions and insights from each of the six restaurant consulting firms I talked to. Going to the pros is a good way to cut risk because they know the pitfalls and potential challenges you might face.

| It takes guts to stand pat too!

Over a six-month period I met with some of the top restaurant consultants in the business. I listened as much as I talked. I'd narrowed it down to two firms that I thought could best manage our Eden restaurant chain. Then I called another meeting and presented all that I'd learned to my partners, including the insights that I'd picked up just from listening to the pros. But based on that information, and a few other matters, we decided to put our restaurant chain on the backburner indefinitely. We simply decided that the risks were too great at that point. We may still do it some day when the market looks right and we aren't all so busy, but it was going to be a tricky deal to pull off because so many of us had strong brands that were already tied to lucrative licensing deals.

I had also picked up signals that revenues at celebrity theme restaurants were beginning to weaken, and my gut told me to pull back. As it turned out, there was a big shakeout and many of them cut back their operations or closed down. I had invested a lot of time and effort in our little slice of Eden, but when I went over my risk/reward balance sheet, it was definitely heavier on the risks. I didn't want to get a lot of other people involved in a business venture built on such an uncertain foundation.

> *When your heart says yes and your gut tells you no, trust your gut.*

This one didn't happen, but in the end, we all walked away feeling good about the experience. We weighed it very carefully. We took our time and did it right. We invested enough time, energy, and money to make certain that we had all of the information that we needed to measure the risks and rewards. And we all agreed that the timing wasn't right but it was great that we all got together and gave it a shot.

3. CHECK THE FACTS AND THEN CHECK YOUR EGO

It's often said that entrepreneurs tend to be egomaniacs, but most of the street-smart successes I know are far more likely to base their decisions on financial figures rather than any ego they've got invested. It wasn't easy for me to admit to all of those other fitness-industry leaders that the timing wasn't right for my Eden restaurant concept, but you can't let pride be your downfall when the risk/reward balance looks bad. Don't get confused. Good decisions aren't made out of pride. Instead, pride is the product of good decisions. (That's *Zen By Jake*, just for you, grasshopper!)

Believe in yourself, but believe in the facts too. Numbers don't lie so, if they don't add up to a profit for your business in a reasonable amount of time, don't take the risk. And if the experts and advisors tell you that the timing isn't right, give their advice serious consideration. They aren't always right, but their experience and their knowledge mean that their opinions deserve your attention.

Check It Out

Here's a risk checklist to help you evaluate whether to take a leap or to go look for another way to grow:

- *Ask yourself why you've come to this "risky" decision.*

Picture the risk you are considering as one of those frayed and wobbly rope bridges across a canyon—the sort of thing my buddy Wiels Spielberg likes to throw in his movies. Before you take a walk on the wild and wobbly side, ask yourself: Why am I about to do this? Was I running after something or running from something?

This is the old pain versus pleasure question. Most decisions we make are either to escape pain or acquire pleasure. As you might expect, the best decisions are those based on reaching for something good rather than running from something bad. Does walking across this high-risk bridge get you where you want to go that much quicker than other, safer routes? Will it help you beat the competition?

> *Run toward opportunities and problems will take care of themselves.*

Remember, it's okay to take risks because you want more for your life, as long as you understand that it's not taking the risk that changes your life, it's the pursuit of goals and dreams that does the trick!

- *Figure out exactly what you hope to accomplish.*

Even Indiana Jones wouldn't run out on that rope bridge without knowing what's on the other end. Well okay, maybe he would if the bad guys with guns were chasing him, but no one is chasing you. So remember that. You aren't running away from anything. Take the time to fully understand what will be accomplished by taking this risk. Though I never advise anyone else to do it, I once took out a second mortgage on our house to finance a business venture. This is back in the early days of our marriage before we had kids, and Tracey, who has a strong business background, encouraged me to do it. Otherwise I never would have taken that kind of risk. But she helped me see that, at that point in our lives, what I thought we could accomplish was worth it. You can't always go by the book and you can't always take the safe route, but you'd better have a clear vision of what you are doing and what your options will be no matter how things work out!

■ *Consider worst-case and best-case scenarios.*

This is about evaluating the potential opportunities that might crop up in either case. It's not about what-if-ing yourself into insanity. Always keep in mind that opportunities aren't limited to best-case scenarios. There are always opportunities even if the worst happens. And the difference between those who make it and those who fail often depends on whether or not they are able to grab new opportunities even when they are flat on their backs. You've always got to be ready to jump in the game and give it your best shot. It might help to keep you alert to opportunities by envisioning yourself as an athlete who keeps the game uniform and shoes out at all times just in case a game breaks out. The important thing is to be in the game because, even if one opportunity proves to be a bust, you'll be ready for the next shot.

| *Stand ready to grab new opportunities.*

Look, not every risky move is going to work out. Expect that. Understand that you are probably going to get your assets handed to you at least once or twice. But know this too: There will be new opportunities waiting whether you soar to the top or fall on your face. So never step onto that shaky bridge of risk without knowing that there will be opportunities even if it starts to break loose. Prepare yourself so that if you get slammed into the side of the mountain, you'll have a plan for scrambling back up and starting over again.

That will cut your risks dramatically and save you all sorts of time and effort later on.

- *Enjoy the thrill ride!*

When you go to the amusement part and get on the roller coaster or the Tower of Terror, you know there are risks involved. Nobody is forcing you to take those risks. Consciously or unconsciously, you've calculated that the rewards are worth the risk. In the case of the amusement park, the reward is the thrill ride. I've got news for you. It's the same in business. Risks are part of the ride, and it's a long run, my friends, so hang on and enjoy the thrills, the spills, and the chills! There are going to be white-knuckle moments when you wonder what the heck you were thinking. There will be times when you think you're going to lose your lunch or go flying out of your seat. You bought the ticket. You knew that being an entrepreneur wasn't going to be as safe and comfortable as working for somebody else. So sit back and enjoy the roller coaster, knowing that you are living the life that you chose for yourself.

> *You knew there'd be risks, so just fasten your seatbelt and enjoy the ride.*

That's what it's all about! Sure, it's easier to enjoy the ups and downs when you've had some success and you feel securely strapped in, but the early tossing and turning is what you'll remember most at the end of your trip. And even to this day, I get a kick out of it when someone asks me, "So Jake, what do you do?" Because as a street-smart entrepreneur, I get to say: "Whatever I want, pal. What*ever* I want!" And so will you!

go to failure and beyond!

IN MY EARLY bodybuilding days, I worked out every day at a California gym where many other professional bodybuilders did their serious lifting. This was no yoga and yogurt hangout. It was a muscle factory, an industrial strength gym dripping with sweat. It sounded like a factory too, but instead of mechanical sounds it echoed with human grunts, bellows, and roars. I'd been pumping iron since high school, so I didn't give a lot of thought back then to something else I heard all the time in that gym and nearly every other one I'd ever been in. It was a phrase used by everybody in the gym to push themselves beyond their limits in order to break down muscle fibers so that they could expand and strengthen them.

"Okay, let's go to failure!" they'd say.

When bodybuilders hear that phrase near the end of a set, it means to keep pumping until you have no strength left. Going to failure is only done with a coach, a trainer, or a friend standing by to "spot" you so they can help with the weight bar or barbells once you've exhausted your muscles. It's such a common phrase in gyms that I never gave it much thought until I got involved in other lines of work and realized that not everyone views "going to failure" as a positive thing, as a way of building strength. Instead, many people are afraid to take risks and fail because they see failure as the end, the finale, the last good-bye. Psychologists will tell you that many people have a great fear of failure because they equate failing with death.

That's one of the silliest fears ever, but I've seen it paralyze very smart and otherwise successful people. I know of one man in particular, a very wealthy and popular Hollywood executive, who was suddenly overcome with the sense that he was a failure even though he'd had great success over a long period of time. He went into a depression and refused to get out of bed for an entire year!

> *Failure isn't fatal. Live it. Learn it. Leave it in the dust!*

Have you ever heard someone say, "I'll just die if this project doesn't work out" or "I'm gonna kill myself if I don't get that job"?

People say those things when, for some crazy reason, they've come to view failure as having the finality of death. That's nuts! Look, if you've got any street smarts at all you know that losing a deal or even going bankrupt isn't death because you get to wake up the next morning and greet a new day. So if you've ever had a tendency to fall apart because of a failure, get the heck over it right now! If you are living and breathing and able to get out of bed, it ain't over! If you don't quit, you will find new opportunities to thrive!

Even the Hollywood executive who let himself be paralyzed by fear finally got out of bed and went back to work. You probably guessed what happened. He knocked out a whole string of more hits for both television and the movies. So, failure has nothing to do with death, does it? In fact, failing is part of living. It's what happens *to* you, not *in* you. That's why failing doesn't mean you are a failure. What would happen if everybody who experienced a failure just gave up and went to bed for a year. Baseball legend Babe Ruth was one of the biggest strikeout kings in the history of the sport, so I guess if he'd given up after every strikeout he would never have also been one of the greatest home-run hitters in the game.

> *There are no strikeouts in business. So keep swinging for the fences!*

I sometimes do live shows on the Home Shopping Network on Sunday mornings when most of America is on the golf course, in church, or sleeping. I'll sneak a peek at the computer screens that track the number of calls coming in to order product, and there may be times when there isn't a single call coming in. I swear, during some of those slack periods, I can hear crickets chirping across the nation, and I feel that no one is watching. But I can't just stop and start to cry and sit in the corner and quit. The show has to go on! Life goes on. Things go in natural cycles and you can't just give up because you are having a bad day, a bad month, or even a bad year.

Even nature has its downtime. Why do you think we have a fall and a winter? They are part of the seasonal cycle. Fall is nature's time to kick back. Winter is when things sleep, store up energy, and wait for Spring to bloom again. (Next book: *Nature Notes By Jake!*)

Up in Smoke

Can failure knock the wind out of you? Sure. Should it absolutely kick your buttisimo? No. *Don't be a wimp!* Some things aren't going to work out. It happens. I could write a book just on my failures. The MegaFlex is one for my loss column. It was a total-body workout machine but it violated one of our major rules: people should be able to comfortably sit down during a workout at home. It didn't demonstrate well on television. It's too bad because the infomercial we did for it had the best theme song ever. (I'd hum it but I'm saving that for the audio book.) In hindsight, we should have just sold the theme song as a single and tried to make our money there. But you know what? We survived!

I've been failing my whole life and I'm still here! I've had products fail, magazines fail, television pilots fail; even my first acting role turned out to be a major Womba bomba! Sometimes, though, you've just got to laugh through the tears.

One of the celebrities I met at the gym when I first moved to L.A. was Tommy Chong, the hippie comedian who was then making hit movies with his partner, Cheech Marin. They had a long-running comedy shtick in which they acted like pot-head wackos. In truth, they are a couple of very sharp, hard-working guys, on top of being hilariously funny whether on stage or in person. I got to be friends with both of them. They always got a kick out of my stories from my days at Universal Studio Tours where I played the Hulk, so they wrote a Hulk-like character into one of their comedies and asked me to take the role. Oddly enough, the movie was called *Cheech & Chong's Next Movie*. The character was this bright red, bumbling superhero called Womba. In the movie script, Womba was always rescuing the wrong people, walking through the wrong wall, and generally causing havoc whenever he tried to do the helpful superhero thing. He was a big red super-klutz.

When Tommy asked me to read the script, I nearly cried, not only because it was so funny but because it was such a great role. It was a big part too. I was going to be billed as a co-star. At that point, I'd never even been on a movie set. This was before I started doing fitness breaks on CNN too, so it was an incredible opportunity. Tommy and the movie producer, Howard Brown, were great to me. They even met with me and my parents, who'd moved to Tarzana, near L.A.

"Mr. and Mrs. Steinfeld, your son Jake is going to be a big star, so be prepared. This is going to be a very big movie," Howard told them.

I was so excited I called all my friends back in Long Island and told them that I was going to be in the next Cheech and Chong movie even before we even started filming. My buddies couldn't believe it! It got even better when the movie got rolling. I had my own little trailer on the set and all the free food I could eat, plus they were paying me a couple of thousand dollars a week to be Womba. What a life!

The first couple days went great. Even the camera guys would start laughing as soon as I walked out wearing red tights with my skin painted red. Then, just as I was heading out the door on the third day of shooting, I got a phone call from the line producer, Peter McGregor Scott.

"Jake, mate, I have some good news and some bad news," he said. "We have been looking at the dailies and the executives at the studio think your work is fantastic but they have a problem. They say that the 245-pound guy painted red dominates every scene you are in. They said they aren't paying to have a 245-pound red guy be the star. They are paying for Cheech and Chong!"

Womba immediately detected trouble! I offered to play the role smaller, maybe in a light chartreuse instead of bright red?

"Jake, I'm sorry, but they've told me to cut Womba from the movie," he said. "The good news is that we will leave you in one scene and you will still be given your full pay. Oh, and you can keep eating with us if you want."

Womba washed up? Womba wimpered. Womba wanted back in his movie! Here I'd told everybody I knew that I was going to be a star in a Cheech and Chong movie and now, I was cut to a red blur in one scene. I felt that I was finished in show business! I sat alone in my apartment for hours staring at my potted plant, which wasn't very sympathetic.

Tommy and Cheech called me as soon as they heard the news. They were more sympathetic than my potted plant, but they also shared some Hollywood wisdom. "This crap happens to everybody, Jake. Don't let it get you down. You've got talent. You'll get another chance!"

It was tough for me to accept that this failure wasn't the grand finale to my acting career, or to my life in general. My friends coached me through it by telling me to focus on the doors that were opening even as that one door (the one with the star on it) was closing.

If you believe the good reviews you'd better believe the bad ones too.

Cheech and Chong were right. It was shortly after Womba got whacked that my celebrity fitness training business really took off. The funny thing was that whenever I told my actor and actress clients the Womba story, they all had similar tales—and usually a couple of them. They'd all been rejected for big roles or cut from movies. They'd all been told that they had the wrong look, a bad nose, a weird voice, or not enough talent for a certain role. In fact, every one of them had experienced failure time and time again.

When I met with Harrison Ford for a workout and told him what happened, he gave me a tip that I've never forgotten. And a reality check.

"If you believe the good reviews you'd better believe the bad ones too, ol' buddy!" Harrison said.

That one sentence has stayed with me my entire career. I realized that "going to failure" was not such a bad place to go because it means you are still out there kicking, struggling, and striving for success. Whether you measure success in terms of magazine covers with your mug on them, annual sales revenues, points on the scoreboard, or good deeds accomplished, you've got to understand that failure is part of the process—not only the success process, but also the process of living! That's something that's stayed with me over the years, and I'm grateful for it. It's not only made me appreciate failure, but I have absolutely no fear of it either.

> *Every great entrepreneur has experienced failure. None of them have been* failures!

When I talk to business school students, I like to shake them up by telling them that when I look out at them, I see one failure after another! That always gets their attention. Then I tell them that they are looking at a guy who has been a failure all of his life. "In fact," I tell them, "all of the great entrepreneurs have been lifelong failures because each and every one of their successes was achieved only after they've gone through failures first."

Sometimes, I even inspire myself!

Success Follows Failure

I truly believe that success is failure turned inside out. When you live and work in Hollywood, you see first-hand that there is no such thing as an overnight success. Instead, you see that success is built upon failure after failure. Many of my "fabulous" celebrity clients identified far more with their spectacular failures because, like weightlifters and bodybuilders, they understood that their failures were the source of their strength and the stepping stones to their successes.

I got to know my famous clients as few others do, as real people. I learned about the obstacles they have had to overcome and the ones they still faced. I saw what drives and motivates them. I realized that nothing comes easy even to those who may make it look easy. Mostly, though, I learned that these people really are not much different from you and me. They've struggled and failed but those that stay on top have learned to accept failures and rejection as part of the process.

I trained Bette Midler early in her acting career. She may be a diva and the Divine Miss M, but she's also a scrappy, driven lady whose strength of determination matches her considerable talent. She can also cuss fluently in several languages! I know, because she unleashed on me during every work-out. Bette is a very street-smart lady and she was one of the clients who told me about her own rejections and failures as a singer and actress. When I began training her, in fact, she'd just been slapped around by the critics for her role in the 1981 movie *Jinxed*. She was feeling beat up, particularly since she had been riding high just two years earlier after being nominated for an Academy Award for her performance in *The Rose*.

Bette was feeling down but she wasn't out. She'd grown up in a family that didn't have a lot. She'd worked her way up to stardom by singing in honky-tonks and raunchy bars. She didn't give up easily.

"Jake baby," she told me, "it can only get better, because it can't get any worse."

Bette had her own take on "go to failure," but it was the same basic philosophy. We both had to laugh when she got her next great movie role, especially because the title was so appropriate. The movie was *Down and Out in Beverly Hills*. The irony of that title was incredible because she starred in it with two other great actors, Nick Nolte and Richard Dreyfuss, who'd also gone through some tough times before they got their roles in it. *Down and Out in Beverly Hills* became a huge hit. It resurrected the careers of all three of the stars and became one of Hollywood's great comeback stories.

I was still training Bette when *Down and Out* hit the theaters. I teased her because a few months earlier I'd noticed that her telephone never rang while we were working out—a rare thing for most of my celebrity clients. But after her new movie started getting rave reviews, the phone at her house rang constantly. We could hardly get in a workout session because of all the studio executives calling her to do their movies.

"What goes around comes around, Jake my man," she told me.

Potholes and Pitfalls

Earlier in the book I stressed that you should always make sure your heart and your mind are committed to any business concept that you want to take to start-up and build your life around. We're now in the fifth year of pumping life into Major League Lacrosse (MLL) and let me tell you, I'm grateful every day that I love this game and the world of sports and fitness because if I didn't, I'd be an absolute nutcase at this point. Don't get me wrong, this has been an experience I wouldn't trade for anything, and every day I see that we are building a great future. But every day is not a great day when you are in a start-up business. I go to failure more as a league owner than I ever did as bodybuilder. My consolation is that, bruise by bruise, day by day, we are getting stronger every day.

> *Trust your friends. Trust the experts. But trust your gut most of all!*

Some days you get kicked around like an old newspaper on the street corner. With the MLL, I've learned that the world of sports has millions of spectator seats and the people in those seats all have opinions and their own ideas about how things could be done better. We welcome their input.

When you start your own business, you will have your critics and arm-chair quarterbacks too. That's just part of the deal. Customers, clients, board members, advisors, family members, competitors, and the guy parking your car will all feel compelled to wonder why you aren't doing this or that, or why you don't have twenty-five teams instead of six. They'll all tell you that you are going to fail.

Smile, nod your head, and stay focused on your own plan. Listen to people you respect, and, in the end, follow your gut instincts. Don't let fans, media critics, or anyone else knock you off your path. It's easy to get caught up in the bullchips but you can't let that bring you down. Sometimes, I think the psychological challenges are tougher than the daily headaches of running a business. Be ready for that, and be ready to deal with it by keeping your focus off your fears and on the long-term plan.

Imagine how difficult it is to run just one sports team, where you are dealing with athletes, staff, scheduling, payroll, marketing, stadiums, fans, and the media. Now multiply that by six, or twelve, because we are in the process of doubling the number of teams in the next couple years. So, it's a good thing we love what we're doing, right? And it's also a good thing that I understand that I'm not going to be the King of the Hill every day of the business week. In fact, in the very beginning stages of any business, even the smartest street-smart entrepreneur is going to find that most days are very humbling.

| *When things get bumpy, fly over the rough spots!*

When we launched the MLL, if there were thirty-five potholes in the road, I hit thirty-seven of them. In the second year, I managed to avoid maybe 25 percent of them. Now, I'm down to hitting maybe 10 or 20 pot-holes a day. Of course, some of them are big enough to swallow a bus, but, hey, at least the numbers are down and I'm working with a great team of guys. The message here is: Know that it isn't going to be easy. Expect to get beat up and bruised on a regular basis, and be willing to take setbacks and failures as part of the daily march toward your dream. Street-smart entrepreneurs don't quit.

Numbers Don't Lie

The Small Business Administration conducted a study of 3,400 entrepreneurs who'd gone bankrupt because of business failure. Twenty-five percent of them said they planned to start another company—immediately. When asked if they would do it all over again and start another business, over 61 percent said they would!

Management psychologist David Weiman told *Business Week* that entrepreneurs in general "have an ability to keep going even when they don't have others standing shoulder to shoulder with them." The magazine cited the case of Phil Holland, who went broke in 1970 after he'd personally backed a restaurant chain that failed. He turned down a management job in a big corporation because, as a true entrepreneur, he wanted to control his own destiny. Obviously, Phil Holland didn't see his failure, as big as it was, as the end of the road. He didn't quit. He was in the hole financially, and so he decided to build a business by putting dough around a hole. He scraped together $5,000 and opened his first Yum Yum Donut Shop in Los Angeles.

It grew to a chain of 138 stores before he sold it in 1989 and used his earnings to become a shopping center magnate!

> *Believe in what you are doing but believe what the numbers are telling you too!*

Okay, I've got you pumped up to have no fear when it comes to failure, but the Surgeon General says I have to paste a warning label on that bit of advice. Having no fear isn't the same as being foolhardy. Experts who counsel bankrupt entrepreneurs say their number one mistake is that they have so much optimism and faith in their own abilities that they don't pay adequate attention to the numbers. That's why we brought in a bottom line watchdog to keep down costs. He makes sure that our prices are high enough and that we are getting paid on time by those who owe us money!

So let's amend my advice to: Have no fear, but stay focused on the financial books! Having a great attitude is wonderful, but keeping good records— and that means doing monthly financial statements—is vital!

Oh, one more thing, don't operate heavy machinery while reading this book. (I think I'm cool with the Surgeon General now.)

Spare Change? Never!

When we first started talking about moving *Body By Jake* out of its very comfortable and lucrative niche as a brand licensing company, I've got to admit, there were moments when I thought, "Why do I want to change a good thing? If it ain't broke, why fix it?"

Fear of change ranks a close second to fear of failure in the list of deadly sins for street-smart entrepreneurs. The business that doesn't change and evolve along with the ever-changing markets, economics, and technologies simply will get left behind by more responsive and innovative competitors. Ask IBM, which had the early technology for creating home computers and laptops but decided to stick with its lucrative and dominant business in massive mainframes for business clients. Then along came Bill Gates of Microsoft and Steve Jobs at Apple and other smaller, quicker, and more innovative companies like Compaq, Dell, and Gateway, and in just a few months, old change-resistant IBM had lost its position as the world's most respected computer company.

Stay focused, but always know what's going on around you.

As the person who leads your company, you have to welcome and lead change by communicating your desire to stay on top of social trends, technologies, and shifting economic circumstances. If *Body By Jake*, which is hardly a high-tech company, hadn't paid attention and jumped on the Internet with an online presence right away, we would never have recaptured those lost sales and the revenues they generated. I saw an opportunity with America's oldest game—one that offered hitting, scoring, and speed. My creation of Major League Lacrosse was in direct response to the social trend of sports fans looking for more affordable and intimate experiences. We picked up on those changes in the business environment by paying attention and through two-way communication. We talked and listened to other entrepreneurs and business leaders as well as to our own employees and, especially, to our customers.

Street-smart entrepreneurs don't forget where they came from—the street. They keep their eyes and ears on what's happening on Main Street USA even if their companies grow to become global giants. You can't run and hide from changing markets, technologies, or social trends, you've got to adapt to them and, hopefully, ride them to new heights. Don't make the common mistake of assuming that your managers and employees or even your top executives are paying attention. Often, they are so caught up in the day-to-day challenges inside the company that they aren't looking out the windows or talking to people on the outside.

It is also *your* responsibility to lead change within the company so that any employees who are afraid of change will get with the program or get out of the way. Understand that the way to get them to buy into change is to first show them the big picture and then explain to them where they fit in. With all of the layoffs and downsizing out there, who can blame them for being afraid of change? So, if you value your employees, you've got to let them know that they have a role in the company's future.

| *Leaders are champions of change.*

Some employees—and some entrepreneurs too—may act out their fear of change by ignoring new instructions, continuing their old ways, and even sabotaging efforts to respond to changing times. If you find yourself, or those who work for you, responding in those ways, you'll need to consider that the alternative to change is usually stagnation and being left behind by the competition.

Start Your Own Traditions and Keep Trading Up

In creating Major League Lacrosse, I decided to make some changes to the way the game would be played. Yeah, I'm the guy who took it upon himself to make major adjustments to the oldest team sport in America! Did I take any flak? Naw, of course not. Well, yeah, I took truckloads of flak from players, coaches, fans, and anybody who'd ever swung a stick in the direction of a lacrosse game, but I had the backing of my partners David Morrow and Tim Robertson. I understand and respect the great traditions of the sport but I believe that even games have to change to compete. Professional basketball, baseball, and football have certainly made adjustments to their uniforms and rules over the years: The three point play and the shot clocks are good examples.

We've tried to create an exciting niche by playing the game in the summer when there is less television competition. We want to give our league a chance to grow and thrive. So, we started by redesigning the jerseys, helmets and equipment. Then, I turned up the change meter by putting in a 45-second shot clock to speed up what many already considered to be the nation's fastest moving sport. Later, we turned back the clock a little by making it a 60-second shot clock. This change was done to keep things moving while maintaining the competitive balance between offense and defense. Then, taking a cue from basketball, we added a two-point arc to open up even greater scoring opportunities.

Our goal is to make this game as exciting as possible for the fans. Oh, we also changed the color of the ball to make it easier for the fans to see it on television and in the bigger stadiums, where we hope to be playing to packed stands! For most of these changes, I trusted Dave Morrow's judgment because he is an important figure in the sport and he really knows the game. He has been right 98 percent of the time. His only problem is in picking Italian restaurants!

Those were major changes to a sport that really values its traditions. There was resistance. We were called a few names by some who didn't like us tinkering with their sport. But one of the keys to leading change in a business is to know not only where you are going, but where you have been. And we knew a little bit about the history of lacrosse. The first report of the sport was written in 1636 and it's changed in many ways over the years. So, when people criticized me for making changes, I simply reminded them that, like most sports that survive over a long period, the rules and style of play have changed continuously over the game's nearly four century history!

I pointed out that when the Algonquin, Kickapoo, Seminole, Bungi, Cherokee, Huron, Passamaquoddy, and other tribes played lacrosse, they didn't exactly sell tickets and refreshments to fans in the stands. They played to entertain their spiritual leaders, honor the dead, improve the weather, heal the sick, train for war, and to settle disagreements between tribes. The French gave the sport its modern name. "Lacrosse" means "the stick." The Algonquin, who apparently had a pretty good sense of humor, reportedly called the game "Baggattaway," which meant "they bump hips," according to one historical account. Other tribes knew it as the "Creator's game" and saw it as a ceremonial battle between good and evil.

| Build on the past for future success.

In the earliest times of American Indian lacrosse, the game had few rules, and they varied widely from tribe to tribe and across the continent. The balls were made of deerskin in most cases, but the types of sticks varied widely. Sometimes the games would last for days, with breaks between sundown and sunset. The playing field could extend several miles with as many as a thousand players, in what resembled warfare more than sport. In the early days, players did not wear protective equipment, or shoes for that matter. One Frenchman who watched the Native American game said, "Almost everything short of murder is allowed."

From a historical perspective, then, lacrosse has changed greatly over the years. It's good to keep history in mind when faced with changing your own business. Everything undergoes change in order to adapt and survive. If you want to get better results than you've been getting, it's only natural that you've got to change what you've been doing. So why is it that so many business owners, not to mention people in general are afraid to make a change so they can make a move to something better?

Like many entrepreneurs, I'm almost a fanatic optimist. I just naturally feel things are going to work out for the best when I decide to make a change. Sometimes I have to take charge and devote huge amounts of time and energy to get that positive result, but I'm willing to do that to enact a positive change. My feeling is that if you are moving the ball forward, then you're winning the game. That's why it is hard for me to understand why people who realize that a change has to be made still are afraid to take those first steps to break away.

No Fear!

Whether your business is struggling, making nice profits, or dominating the market, the owner—that would be you—has to be willing to get the others in his company to buy into the change. Why? Because everything that impacts your business is in a constant state of change. If your business isn't changing, it will be overtaken and left behind by competition that is willing to adapt to changing economics, technologies and markets. As a street-smart entrepreneur, you and your company should have an advantage. In most cases, if your business is small, you will be able to respond more quickly to shifting conditions. Larger companies and corporations tend to be more bureaucratic and therefore slower to react and more resistant to change

I encourage you to create a culture within your company that sees change as simply a part of doing business. To help you build that culture, here are a few basic rules for helping you and your employees overcome the fear of change:

1. IT IS ABOUT SURVIVAL

Street-smart entrepreneurs don't chase fads or trends. They make major changes in order to grow and survive over the long-term so that the company will continue to make profits and keep employees on the payroll. Keep in mind that the first thing you may have to change is yourself. Most entrepreneurial companies reflect the personalities of their creators and their driving force. When we reinvented *Body By Jake* into a global fitness and media company, we brought in additional employees. That meant I had to learn to delegate more, listen more, and stay out of the way of the experts I'd hired.

> *You might have to change yourself before you can change your business!*

I also had to learn to communicate our goals and the purpose of changes to them. With any change it is essential that you make the purpose clear by setting measurable performance goals to show how changes help the company over the long term.

2. IT IS ABOUT YOUR COMPANY *AND* YOUR EMPLOYEES

If you expect your employees to buy into a change and to go with the flow, you've got to show them how it will benefit them, especially if their jobs are going to change. Some people might have to shift to jobs they don't want. Others may lose their jobs. Don't expect them to buy into it if it is obviously going to have a negative effect. Give them the option of leaving and make it as painless as possible without hurting your business.

3. LISTEN TO THOSE WHO RESIST CHANGE

As you already know, I'm a big believer in following my gut instincts, but I also know what I don't know. I am surrounded by smart people in all of my enterprises, so I listen to them when they don't agree with me, including when they question changes that I want to make in my businesses. Some people fear change and resist it instinctively, but sometimes they have good reasons.

> *If your employees are resisting change, listen and understand before you respond.*

If you hire talented people, you owe it to them, and to yourself, to listen to them when they resist change. They might just help you change for the better. The fact that you listen to them will make your company stronger for the long haul, which is really the point of any change.

4. IT'S BETTER TO GET A BUY-IN THAN TO DRAG THEM IN

You are a leader only if people are willing to follow you. There is a difference between forcing change and leading it. Corporations often have "change agents" who ram changes down the throats of employees, who accept it—but only because they want to keep their jobs. Those employees are not likely to perform at high levels, and they are far less likely to accept future changes. They may even secretly try to screw up things so the changes fail. Experts say it's best to lead change by creating a culture or environment in which each employee feels a part of the plan, and each understands how he or she will benefit over the long term. If you show your employees that there is a better way that will help them grow with the company, then that sense of security will help them accept change.

5. DON'T GET CUTE

Your employees may grow cynical and resistant to change efforts that are oversold as the next great thing or as the ultimate cure for all that ails your business. Remember, you want a culture in which change is accepted as part of doing business. It's not a crusade, it is *business*. Don't get righteous about it. Be honest that it's not going to be easy and that some people aren't going to be as comfortable. Routines will be thrown off, unforeseen problems will undoubtedly occur. But let them know that you are all in this together and as long as they are loyal to the company, you will be loyal to them.

| *Nothing endures like change.*

When you step back and take the long view, the fears we often have about change or risk seem almost silly. But up close, with the future of your business on the line, they can seem very real. So keep in mind that taking risks and making changes are as much a part of business as opening in the morning and closing at night. Be ready to take risks. Be willing to make changes. Street-smart success requires that you do both! Remember, no fear! One of my favorite sayings is:

> There are those who fail but get back up, lose but don't accept loss, and succeed because they will not fail. These people don't teach by words, they inspire by example!

10

don't quit giving back!

THE "DEAR JAKE" letter came from a science teacher at a high school in Brooklyn. He described himself as the type who wears a bow tie and a button-down shirt to work every day. He started out by saying that he'd really been inspired by my speech at his school. I do a lot of those presentations because of my most enjoyable street-smart enterprise of all—the Don't Quit! Foundation. It is a charitable organization I started to make a real difference. We give fitness centers to schools across the country. Before the ribbon-cutting ceremonies, I always do a little presentation in the auditorium. I challenge the students and the teachers to use the tools that we've given them to build both their bodies and their self-confidence.

This teacher from Brooklyn wrote to tell me that he had accepted that challenge and benefited in ways that he'd never expected. He wrote that his students had always been a little intimidated by his scholarly appearance and the subject he taught until he began running on the treadmill alongside his students in his school's new fitness center.

You see, this guy in the bow tie was also an athlete and a marathon runner, but his students had never seen that side of him before.

"I went into the gym and got on the treadmill one day and these five kids said, "You are like Superman on that treadmill!"

His students suddenly saw the chemistry teacher in an entirely new light. It gave them a new respect for him, and a way to relate to him.

"Jake, from that point on, I had five new friends at the school, and five kids who never missed another class because they had learned to see their teacher as a regular guy who cared about their futures."

I gotta tell you, that's one of the things I really hoped would happen when I decided that it was time to give something back by giving fitness centers to inner city high schools and middle schools around the country.

Street-smart entrepreneurs are also smart about finding ways to make a difference in their communities. It makes sense from a business perspective, and it makes life better for you, your employees and your customers.

As a former chubby kid who has built his life around health and fitness, I get upset when I read articles or hear news reports about obesity in young people. It makes me want to do more to reach kids and get them on a healthier track. I hope you get that emotionally involved in whatever your chosen entrepreneurial field happens to be. And, in this final chapter, I want to encourage you to commit to an even deeper form of involvement. I want you to think about giving something back too.

I'm not saying you have to become Mother Teresa, but there is something every entrepreneur can do—and you might be surprised at the benefits you and your business will reap when you re-invest some of your profits—or your time, effort, and knowledge—in the community and world around you. Many social service agencies and charities are hurting because of cuts in government support, so this is a great time to step up. I'd like you to do it because it's the right thing to give back, but it also makes good business sense to share the wealth.

| *Giving back to your community pays huge dividends!*

From personal experience, I can tell you that many of the best business contacts I've ever made have been through my involvement in philanthropy and charities. Other entrepreneurs and business leaders appreciate those who reach out and give a helping hand to the needy. And they can show their appreciation in some very impressive ways! Philanthropy pays unexpected dividends, take it from me. I've had as much fun giving away things as I've had selling them, even more. And the networking I've done through my charity has benefited my business greatly.

Even if your business is just getting off the ground, I encourage you to look around and see where you can make a difference. Don't go for the old cop-out: *What can one person do?* I'm not asking you to save the world. But if everybody does just a little, think of the difference it could make! There are all sorts of ways you can use your talents, knowledge and your time to benefit others. You don't have to be Bill Gates to share the wealth, but the man from Microsoft is a good example. The Bill and Melinda Gates Foundation is probably the ultimate in entrepreneurial philanthropy. It has more than $27 billion in assets and gives away $1.2 billion a year to libraries, schools, and health organizations, among other causes.

Hey, it's all relative, right? Even if your business is still struggling to get off the ground, you can volunteer for local charities and nonprofits, like Big Brothers/Big Sisters, the YMCA/YWCA, the Boy Scouts or Girl Scouts, or Habitat for Humanity, just to name a few. Once you've made your fortune, or enough to be comfortable, you might consider starting your own nonprofit foundation to do good deeds that matter to you and your community. Give back thoughtfully, don't just throw money out there and think you are making a difference. Remember the old saying, that instead of handing out tuna sandwiches, it's better to teach people to fish so that they can feed themselves! (Did I get that right? Or was it grouper instead of tuna?)

Todd Wagner created the Todd R. Wagner Foundation after his entrepreneurial start-up, Broadcast.com, had the biggest one-day gain in the history of Wall Street when he was only thirty-eight years old. Of course, he felt incredibly grateful after becoming a multimillionaire overnight. He also put some thought into how he wanted to give back. He decided that entrepreneurs are uniquely qualified to share their business skills with nonprofits, and to help them operate more efficiently so they can reach more people. He calls it "social entrepreneurialism," and it entails an investment of time and skill rather than just money. His foundation works with minority-owned technology start-ups to "equalize the power of technology" by funding their efforts. He also helped create a neighborhood technology center in southern Dallas that provides free Internet access and training.

Bea Salazar didn't make millions overnight, or even over many years, but she has made a difference by whipping up and handing out peanut-butter-and-jelly sandwiches. The founder and president of the nonprofit Bea's Kids, in Carrollton, Texas, was feeling depressed after undergoing back surgery and going on disability. Then, one summer afternoon, she saw a little boy digging in a dumpster near her home. He was looking for food, he told her. She made him a peanut-butter-and-jelly sandwich and sent him home. A few minutes later, she heard a knock at the door and found six more kids in search of a sandwich. They told her that their parents were working and there was no one home to feed them. She got out the bread, peanut butter, and jelly and went to work—and she hasn't stopped. Her landlord saw the need so he gave her the use of an empty apartment. Now ten years old, her nonprofit not only feeds around 100 latch-key kids every day but also helps them with homework. More than 500 children have benefited from her charitable work.

Whether it's because you see a need in your neighborhood, or a world away, every entrepreneur needs to stay connected. Reaching out to others through philanthropy is a great way to do it. I have plenty to be grateful for. For a guy who came from a middle-class family and never got a college degree, I've had an incredible amount of success. I've worked hard and hustled, but I've also benefited greatly from people who have helped me—those who've invested in my products and services—and from living in a country that truly does make it possible for anyone to rise above their circumstances and build a great life!

| *Make the effort to make a difference!*

I've always been available for charity events, especially anything that encourages kids to get off the couch and be more active. In recent years, there have been many articles about the decline in physical fitness programs in schools. There have been reports of rising levels of obesity in children and just a lot of other bad news about kids, their eating habits, and their increasing tendency to spend more time playing video games and watching television instead of playing sports and doing healthier activities.

The news today isn't much better by the way. Nearly 80 percent of the nation's schools have no daily physical education classes. Obesity rates for kids age 6 to 15 are about 30 percent. The number of overweight and obese children continues to rise each year, even with as much as $7 billion being spent to fight this problem. In fact, the number of overweight children doubled from 1980 to 2000. By 2003, fully 15 percent of youngsters age 6 to 18 years were overweight, up from 11 percent just a year earlier.

These kids are at risk for all sorts of health problems that are showing up in younger and younger patients, such as type 2 diabetes, high blood pressure, sleep apnea, and elevated cholesterol levels. This is serious stuff also because adult health problems are rooted in childhood. An obese child is more likely to become an obese adult, which increases the chance for a shorter life span, according to Dr. Carden Johnston, president of the American Academy of Pediatrics.

There's been a lot of criticism recently that programs aimed at reducing obesity in young people focus on educational material rather than on actually changing the lifestyles that lead to weight and health problems. That fact struck me because I'm results-oriented. You can throw millions and millions of dollars at a problem, but if all that money isn't being used effectively, it's just a waste of greenbacks. I don't believe in just doing things for appearance's sake.

I'd been thinking about that problem too, starting back in 1998 when I was doing a series of appearances at health fairs. I'd go and give a little rap-a-doo on fitness, sign some autographs, talk to folks, and pose for pictures with them. It was very enjoyable, but at the end of the day, I'd go home wondering if I'd really done anything to change the life of even a single person I'd seen or talked to that day. Often, I'd get in the car and drive away with the feeling that all I'd left behind for the kids were some free T-shirts, a sack lunch, a few memories, and some medals that they might want to trade for a video game a couple of days later.

Pro Philanthropy

Tracey has a real interest in doing things that change peoples' lives, and she challenged me one day, as only a wife can, to make a real difference after I told her that I wondered if the health-fair appearances were having much of a long-term impact. That's when I first looked into finding some way to make a real difference in the lives of young people whose fitness and health weren't what they should be. One of the things I've preached to street-smart entrepreneurs is to know what you don't know—and then find someone who does know what you don't know! So, I reached out to someone with tremendous expertise in both the health and fitness arena, and in the field of philanthropy.

Her name is Judith Kieffer. She is a lawyer and marathon runner, who was then a member of the President's Council for Fitness and Sports. Judith is also an expert on the creation and operation of charitable foundations. She has worked in the field for many years. She knows what works and doesn't work. And she knows how to set up charitable organizations so that they have a real impact.

| *Charity pros can help you give* the most for your money!

I recruited Judith to run the Don't Quit! Foundation. My goal was very simple—to give young people the tools to build healthier lifestyles and greater self-confidence. But simplicity isn't an easy thing to pull off. And you'd be amazed at how hard it is to give away something, even if it is very beneficial! Fortunately, there are people like Judith as well as many helpful organizations out there to guide you in the process of giving back to your community thoughtfully and effectively.

The mission of my nonprofit Don't Quit! Foundation is to create an environment that supports and educates young people so they can get fit both physically and mentally. We do this by giving inner city middle schools and high schools their own fully-equipped Don't Quit! Fitness Centers. It's a pretty simple concept, and that's the beauty of it. We work with Cybex and Flex fitness equipment manufacturers, who cut us a great deal on the cost of a first-class lineup of weight machines, free weights, three treadmills, five exercise bikes, and other cardiovascular equipment—worth $100,000 total. Once a school is selected, we work with them to find a room or building on campus. Then we handle the details, such as finding contractors to put mirrors on the walls. We also bring in a high-density flooring system that we can teach the students to install like a big puzzle. We also have the school select student artists to do the decorating by putting their school colors, logos, and mascots on the walls alongside our own *Body By Jake* and Don't Quit! Foundation emblems.

It's such a great deal for the schools that it sometimes is tough to convince them that there are no strings attached—but there aren't! Our intention is just to give the schools and the people in them the tools to better themselves and the places they live. This is all about building up students and their teachers too, motivating and inspiring them so that they'll have the inner and outer strength to make their own contributions down the road. Once we move in all of the equipment, give them a cardio-vascular program to get things started, and cut the ribbons at a brief ceremony, we're outta there and it's all theirs! In just five years, we've put Don't Quit! Fitness Centers into twenty-eight schools in California, Washington, District of Columbia, New York, Maryland, Pennsylvania, Ohio, Texas, Florida, Michigan, and the island of St. Thomas—with even more on the way!

I'd love to have 2800 of them some day. We target communities and schools that could never afford their own first class fitness centers, and it's really exciting for me to see the kids and teachers walk in for the first time and check out the Cybex and Flex equipment. Often, they are shocked that everything is brand new. Many of these kids have always dealt with hand-me-downs, whether it's used books or their brother's gym shoes. So the sight and smell of a brand-new fitness center always makes them smile. Me too! Many of our schools report that truancy rates have dropped because only those students who have good attendance records can use the centers.

Fitness centers really are the gift that keeps on giving. I go to every opening at each and every one of them. It's always a terrific, rewarding experience, but I've gotta tell you, the best part is that when we leave, the benefits continue to flow to the young people, the teachers, and the community. The other element that makes this a rewarding way of giving back is that the $50,000 cost for each fitness center comes from a donor. Often, but not always, these donors are businesses or individuals who live in or came from the area.

While we've had great luck in getting corporations like General Motors, TCI, and other companies to contribute to the program, we've also had some really enthusiastic participation from entrepreneurs and their companies.

Some individual donors are even alumni of the schools. Many are my friends and business associates who love the idea of doing something that has a direct impact on the lives of young people.

I don't want to go all Stuart Smiley on you—that's Al Franken's gig. But I've found that when other street-smart successes hear about simple but effective charitable efforts like the Don't Quit! Fitness Centers, they want to lock arms and sing Kumbaya. But more importantly, they buy into it in a big way. Often, in a really big way! Every single donor who has supported one of our fitness centers has come back and done another one, and sometimes several more.

My Dallas dynamo literary agent, Jan Miller of Dupree Miller Literary Agency, told her husband Jeff Rich about the Don't Quit! Fitness Centers. Jefferson, as I call him, is an athlete who still plays in an adult hockey league—oh, and he is also CEO of ACS, a $4 billion Fortune 500 information technology company with 40,000 employees around the world. Yeah, you might say Jefferson is a pretty street-smart guy, and he's already chipped in to build four Don't Quit! Fitness Centers because he loves the concept so much.

My longtime buddy Frank Marshall, the producer of *Sixth Sense, Seabiscuit, The Bourne Identity,* and many of Steven Spielberg's movies, is another big supporter, as is the producer Steve Tisch (*Alex and Emma, Forrest Gump*). It was Frank Marshall who introduced me to two of our most avid supporters, Warren "Pete" and Hillary Musser of Philadelphia. Pete is the founder of Safeguard Scientific, which develops and operates technology businesses. One of the things that works in our favor—and something you should consider when doing philanthropy with your own business—is that donors enjoy seeing where their money goes, and how it benefits people. When our donors attend a ribbon cutting ceremony or come back to visit a Don't Quit! Fitness Center that they've supported, they find the kids and teachers working out together, getting fit and doing something that builds self confidence.

You can't beat it when a donor can see and feel and talk to people about the benefits of the place! People just get it immediately and they buy into it! I met Pete Musser in 1998 when he wanted to donate a Don't Quit! Fitness Center in the name of Frank Marshall because they'd done an IMAX film together on the Olympics. I didn't meet Pete until the dedication ceremony.

He seemed like a great guy. Still when he turned to me and said, "I want to do twenty more of these," I thought he was pulling my leg. But then he called me in L.A., the next week and said he wanted to have lunch to talk about doing more fitness centers with us.

| *Partner up and give twice as much as you get!*

We had the lunch and I still wasn't sure he would really follow through until he had me come to his office in Philadelphia. I went to a 7 A.M. managers' meeting with him and a dozen of his top executives. The first thing he said was, "I just did a Don't Quit! Fitness Center with Jake, and they are incredible. I want each of my managers to do one too. If you don't raise your hand to do one, I'll just take it out of your paychecks!"

Naturally, all twelve hands went up. (Don't worry, these guys could afford it!) Next, Pete asked me to say a few words. History will note that this was one of the few times in my life when I was absolutely speechless. I stood up, cleared my throat, said "Thank you!" and sat down. In a few weeks, I had the checks! I wish it was always that easy! I've learned a few things about entrepreneurial philanthropy from Judith and our experiences with the Don't Quit! Foundation. These tips will help you in your efforts to give back:

Street-Smart Entrepreneurial Philanthropy

1. MAKE IT MATTER!

Whether you donate to an existing charity or start your own charitable organization, I encourage you to put your heart as well as your money into it. Make it matter!

If you've got a family-car business that has thrived in a community or region, then find a way to provide scholarships to the needy kids of your customers who might want to own their own auto dealerships or repair shops some day—or maybe you could endow a rehabilitation center for the victims of automobile accidents. The founder or partners of a successful law firm might give back by creating a nonprofit that funds a free legal clinic for those who might not be able to afford an attorney themselves. Philanthropy isn't just for the ultra-rich and the Hollywood famous. It's for anyone who believes in sharing the rewards of street-smart entrepreneurship. When you put your money back into the community, you not only help others, you draw attention to the issues that you care about and you encourage others to care too!

| *Invest in the future of your community.*

Building fitness centers for needy kids has meant a whole lot more to me than just throwing money at a problem that someone else has identified. I'm glad to do that, of course, but I just find it more rewarding to be involved in a charity that resonates with me personally. Fitness is not a fad or a hobby for me; it is truly my life's work. It's made me what I am today. I couldn't imagine what kind of person I would be if I hadn't finally picked up that curl bar my Dad gave me. I remember the exact moment I did that, and I remember how I felt about myself before I took control, first of my physical health, and then my mental health. It's funny because I carry that self-image around with me. I was a fat kid with a stuttering problem that made it tough for me to talk to anyone, even when I was dying to do it.

Guess what happens whenever I go into a school to open a Don't Quit! Fitness Center? I always find myself looking for the same type of kid. Chubby, insecure, and—it's amazing—I can usually find one with my old hair style too! I immediately attach myself to those kids and I do everything I can to encourage them to give the equipment a try—and to keep at it. Most kids are eager to find ways to help themselves, so if you give them the tools and encourage them to use them, they'll likely jump on the opportunity. It may take them a while to do that, but once they start to see results, miracles can happen. I've seen it happen many times since to other young people who become avid users of our Don't Quit! Fitness Centers.

There are a lot of programs out there to develop the minds of needy young people, but if a kid doesn't have a certain level of self-confidence, you'll never get him or her to sign up. That's why increasing physical fitness is such a great thing. I see myself in the young people who use our fitness centers. That makes the Don't Quit! Foundation personally rewarding for me. I encourage you to build your philanthropy around something that means just as much to you.

2. LEARN HOW TO GIVE THE STREET-SMART WAY

Take the time to understand how effective philanthropy works, even if you hire a pro to set up your program for you. You should understand the differences, as well as the advantages and disadvantages of private foundations versus public charities. The tax laws governing charities give me a two-day headache and make me once again grateful for my long-time legal eagle, Robert "Bob" Lieberman, and for my philanthropy wizard, Judith Kieffer.

Normally, it takes at least $250,000 to set up an endowment, but even that's not going to generate a whole lot of revenue unless you've got a real knack for investing. There are also donor-advised funds that are administered by community foundations; those give you a little more flexibility while handling the day-to-day administration and keeping costs down. Many banks and other financial institutions will also help you set up and manage a charity through a community foundation. You can find a list of community foundations at the Web sites for The Grantsmanship (www.tgci.com) and for the Foundation Center (www.fdncenter.org). Both of those Web sites also provide all sorts of information that will help you create and support your philanthropic adventures.

The easiest way for regular folks to set up a charity is to do what we did for the Don't Quit! Foundation. It is set up as a 501(c)(3), which sounds a little like a Star Wars character but is really one of the most common forms of nonprofit charitable corporations. The name comes from the section of the IRS code that lays out the requirements and qualifications for this type of organization. It has to be devoted to charitable, scientific, religious, or educational purposes. Many clubs, churches, private foundations, and other groups set up as 501(c)(3)s, because once you qualify for this status with the IRS, the corporation can't be taxed. This type of nonprofit is allowed to receive tax free contributions. Even better, donors to these nonprofits can deduct their contributions from their personal tax returns.

| *Find the best way to give and give it the best you can!*

If you need to raise all or some of the money to support your nonprofit, do-good efforts, there are community foundations to lend a hand, but it gets a bit more complicated when you are asking other people to chip in. You may have to set up a separate foundation and pay for consulting advice on how to do it, because rules for incorporating foundations vary from one state to another. Most states require that you form a corporation; this is fairly easy to do, but you'll want a lawyer to check it out to make certain you've done it correctly. Otherwise you may not be eligible to receive tax-deductible donations, according to IRS rules. You will also have to apply for recognition as a tax-exempt entity under federal tax laws. That's when you'll need good ol' IRS form 1023. You'll find a lot of tax information at www.irs.gov. Look for a publication called "Tax Exempt Status for My Organization" (also known as Publication 557). It offers a heap of help.

You will need to do a business plan for your charitable organization because you have to document that you have a budget that shows where your money is coming from for the first three years. The laws governing private foundations are pretty tough because they want to prevent people from being tricked into giving money to charities that only benefit the people running them. So be ready to deal with a lot of red tape if you do it on your own. To protect consumers, fundraisers have to register with the state office in charge of such matters, which is usually the Secretary of State's office.

You can find help and information about that sort of thing at the Web site for the Unified Registration Statement (URS), which helps nonprofit charitable organizations meet state requirements. It's run by the National Association of State Charities Officials and the National Association of Attorney Generals, so they'll give you the straight stuff. Check it out at www.multistatefiling.org.

Thankfully, there are plenty of resources out there to help you navigate your way through the maze of philanthropy start-ups. The Council on Foundations (www.cof.org) is one of the best.

Here are others:

- Association of Small Foundations (www.smallfoundations.org)

- The Philanthropic Initiative (www.tpi.org)

- The Internet Nonprofit Center (www.nonprofits.org)

- The National Council of Nonprofit Associations (www.ncna.org)

3. KEEP IT SIMPLE FOR YOU AND FOR THE BENEFICIARIES

Giving something away can be more complicated than you'd think. When Judith and I contact a school and tell them that we are considering donating a fitness center to their students, it is sometimes a real challenge to get them to take us seriously! Judith is very savvy in understanding how school systems and other big organizations work. She understands that administrators often are afraid of charitable gifts, because they can add to their workloads by creating more bureaucratic burdens without providing funds for additional staff. With that in mind, we always have to assure school superintendents and principals that our fitness centers can be operated by one or two faculty, student, or community volunteers.

| *Smart philanthropy benefits everyone involved!*

Judith says it's amazing how many schools and other agencies will turn down charitable gifts because they don't have the resources to support them year after year. Let's say someone wants to fund a new library building for a school. That's great, except the school still has to come up with the money for books, furniture, and staffing year in and year out. Still, with cutbacks in government funding for physical education, we've never had a school say "no thanks" to a fitness center that serves all students—not just athletes. We do provide the schools with cardiovascular and weight-training programs if they want to work them into their physical education courses, but we don't make any demands or complicate their lives. We just give them the tools and tell them to have fun!

Many schools have tremendous needs but they also face huge piles of local, state, and federal regulations. You may walk in the door thinking you're giving them something wonderful and administrators may be grateful, but they also understand that your gift may come with a lot of additional work for them and their already overworked staffs. The key to giving wisely is to make certain your gift doesn't create a burden for the recipient. We work with each school to make certain that our fitness centers fit seamlessly with their budgets, staffing, and scheduling so that they derive the full benefit at very little extra cost in terms of labor and money.

4. KEEP ADMINISTRATIVE COSTS TO A ROCK-BOTTOM MINIMUM

Judith is the only paid staffer at the Don't Quit! Foundation, and she is paid as a consultant. We don't have any additional office or infrastructure expense. The idea is to make certain that nearly everything we do pays a direct benefit to the school and its students, not to anyone else involved. One of the primary criticisms of charitable organizations is that far too much money goes toward their administrative costs. Don't let that happen to your charity or foundation! Run it like you would run your business, keeping a close eye on the bottom line.

5. SPREAD THE WORD

During every ribbon-cutting ceremony for our fitness centers, we talk to the faculty and the students about philanthropy and giving back to the community. We want the students in particular to understand where the fitness centers come from and why we think it is important to share our success with them. It's also important to get the word out in the community by contacting the media and inviting them to your opening ceremonies or presentation events. This isn't something you do to blow your own horn, it's a way of showing that there are needs that can be served through entrepreneurial philanthropy.

| *Celebrate the spirit of giving!*

Often it's sad but true that with the media "what bleeds leads," meaning that bad news gets more attention than good news. Your challenge is to show the local media representatives that good news sells too! Find an angle that will interest them and their readers, viewers, or listeners by honing in on the local recipients who will benefit from your gift, rather than expecting them to focus on your philanthropy.

6. PLAY THE CORPORATE CARD

The Don't Quit! Foundation has benefited from the corporate giving programs at General Motors, TCI, ACS, and several other major corporations. You may have to jump through hoops to hook up with them and win them over, but once you've been approved, these corporate partners can be a boon to your charitable organization.

Most major corporations have philanthropic programs, with money set aside for doing good deeds in the communities they serve. Don't be shy about making presentations to corporation executives. Encourage them to be your partner in your giving programs. Show them how you can help them by providing a structure that makes it easy for them to give back. And show them the benefits their business will derive from it!

Two Final Words

Body By Jake Inc. was just starting up when a giant sneaker-maker contacted me one day and tried to buy one of my greatest assets. They wanted to buy my trademarked motto: *Don't Quit!* But I wasn't selling. I'll never sell the rights to those two words. They've taken me a long, long way and seen me through some very challenging times. They still get me out of bed in the morning and keep me pushing to start grand new enterprises, like Major League Lacrosse. I'd never sell them out to another company, but I don't mind sharing them with you. They mean a lot to me because they've been with me a long time. I hooked up with them back in the eighth grade at Baldwin Junior High School.

| *Give it all you've got!*

I was chunky, sure, but I had game! So I tried out for the basketball team. I felt pretty confident that I'd make the team, and so I was shocked when they posted the roster and my name was nowhere to be found. It was a blow because even though I was overweight and had a speech impediment, I still thought of myself as a jock. It was so embarrassing; I couldn't even face myself in the mirror.

But then a few days after the team roster was announced, a girl who lived down the street tried to cheer me up by giving me a poem. I wasn't too thrilled with getting a poem at first. I thought maybe she was trying to tell me that I should give up sports and try out for the Dead Poets Society or something. But this girl had a lot of sense, so I read the poem and it changed my life. It's not Emily Dickinson. It's not even Bob Dylan. But it's still on my desk to this day and it's gotten this street-smart entrepreneur through a lot of long days and nights.

You'll probably not be surprised to learn that it's called "Don't Quit!"

When things go wrong as they sometimes will
When the road you're trudging seems all uphill
When the funds are low and the debts are high
And when you want to smile, but you have to sigh
When care is pressing you down a bit
Rest if you must, but do not quit.

Life is queer, with its twists and turns
As every one of us sometimes learns.
And many a failure turns about
When he might have won had he stuck it out.
Don't give up, though the pace seems slow.
You may succeed with another blow.

Success is failure turned inside out—
The silver tint of the clouds of doubt.
And you never can tell how close you are—
It may be near when it seems so far.
So stick to the fight when you are hardest hit.
It's when things seem worst that you must not quit.

So, don't quit! Ever!
Not even when others say that your business idea is not so grande, that no one will ever pay more than a buck for a cup of coffee!

Starbucks is steaming!

Not even when the whole infrastructure of the industry is in turmoil: Kids aren't willing to pay for music any more because they can download it for free!

iTunes rocks!

Not even when they claim other yahoos own the market: There are already enough search engines out there!

Google rolls!

Not even when . . . (insert the challenges your own start-up faces here)!

Street-smart entrepreneurs never quit!

In this book, I've given you many tools to help you be the boss. I know that your street smarts have increased in reading it. More importantly, I hope you've found the spirit of street-smart entrepreneurship in these pages. That's why I've shared with you the enjoyment I get out of being an entrepreneur and providing for my family by doing what I love day in and day out. Be the boss! It's the only way to work and to live.

Stay street smart!

And remember this: *I've seen a lot of famous people naked and they've got nothing on you!*

Believe it. Now go out and achieve it!

Don't Quit!

the naked epilogue

What? You thought that was it?

Did you forget I'm the *Don't Quit* guy?

While you've been reading, I've been doing what street-smart entrepreneurs do. I've been dreaming up new business ideas, working on business plans, refining concepts, making phone calls, and knocking on doors. And before I let you go, I just had to tell you about the latest, greatest deal I've got going. It's a particularly sweet one because I had so many doors slammed in my face before I finally got my foot in one.

I wanted to tell you about it as one final real-world, streetwise example of what happens when you refuse to hear the *No*'s. This deal again offers proof I'm not just preaching that. I practice it. And I live it.

When someone tells me *No*, I actually translate it to *Yes* in my mind! That way I can smile, thank the person, and then get my buttissimo out the door as quickly as possible so I can keep looking for a real *Yes*!

| *When someone tells you* **No,** *turn it into a* **Yes.**

That *Don't Quit!* attitude pays off in big ways. In this case, the sky is the limit. I am unbelievably excited to report to you that after more than five years of working my way through 755,000 *No*'s, I am now preparing to relaunch a new state-of-the-art version of FitTV, my health and fitness television network.

I got a *Yes!* I've got an incredible concept! And I've got an out-of-this-world partner!

I'd like to introduce you to Exercise TV!, an on-demand health and fitness network presented in partnership with Comcast, the nation's largest cable firm! This is a state-of-the-art deal because the way we watch television is going to change rapidly and in a big way. We will soon be able to create our own "networks" with our own favorite shows lined up and ready to go whenever we want to watch them. That is what Exercise TV! is all about. It is a video-on-demand television service. In essence, it is a virtual television network. Using your television remote, you will be able to choose from a whole range of programs on your television. You can click on Exercise TV! We'll offer any kind of workout you want to do at the level that is right for you—from light warm-ups to intense all-out killer workouts!

We'll offer strength training, Pilates, yoga, weight training for men and women, and sports instruction for lacrosse, basketball, soccer, volleyball, football and any other activity you want to get in shape for. There will also be on-demand programming offering motivational and inspirational talks and interviews.

Like I said, the sky is the limit on what we can offer! That's what I love about this. As an entrepreneur I find that the most exciting businesses are those that open the door to all sorts of new enterprises down the road. Exercise TV! does exactly that!

Think about this: Exercise TV! will offer a virtual community in which you will be able not only to find the workouts and health-and-fitness guidance you want, but also to interact over the Internet with other viewers as well as with me. Not only that but this new forum will allow me to introduce the next generation of fitness stars. Who knows, you might be one of them?

Once we're up and running you'll never need to leave your house to buy another workout DVD or video. You'll be able to order up a show from us and create your own library. We'll be your source of all things interesting, fun, new, and healthy! We'll provide the content for Exercise TV! based on what our viewers want. It'll be your network, really, but the *Body By Jake* brand will guarantee quality and customer satisfaction.

I have a large equity stake in this venture. I'm putting to use my brand, expertise, on-air presence, and ability to get sponsors and deal with the affiliate relations folks. I'll keep the team together and motivated to make sure we eventually get into 30 to 40 million homes. Our goal is to corner the market on the health and fitness niche with video-on-demand programming.

This is the next generation of FitTV. It's very different and that's a good thing! The lesson for you is this: As an entrepreneur you have to keep reinventing yourself and what you do! Whether you are a raw rookie in the business world or a battle-scarred veteran, you have to keep pushing the envelope to make sure you are always at the forefront and on top of your game. It might sound corny but the second you start looking back, someone will pass you. You need to stay in physical and mental shape—always knowing and believing that you can achieve anything you want!

> *Stay in the game because you never know when they'll ask you to bat.*

Don't be afraid to buck the system and don't be afraid of the word *No*. When someone tells you *No*, turn on your BBJ auto-translator and turn it into a *Yes!* Then do the Jake-away. Smile, thank them, and get out the door so you can find that *Yes!*

The story of the creation of Exercise TV! is a book in itself, but I'll try to give you the Cliff's Notes version because you are going to face the same sort of challenges. I've been working on creating a new health and fitness network almost since the day we sold FitTV. By 1999, I had targeted the cable market because I saw that the future was in on-demand programming. I've been working in the cable business since 1982, when Ted Turner signed me to do *Fitness Breaks by Jake* vignettes on his startup network. I know many of the movers and shakers in the cable business, including Fred Dressler, who has been a friend and supporter since 1993.

Before he became executive vice president for Time Warner Cable in 2001, Fred was the senior vice president for programming there, which made him the gatekeeper and the guy for me to see. So way back in 1999, I pitched him the idea of a digital service offering. He loved it but he was straight with me. He said there was something in the works that wouldn't allow him to make a move on the idea for a while. He told me to get back to him in a couple months.

Of course, it turned out that he was talking about the merger of Time Warner with AOL, which happened in January of 2000. Naturally, I waited for things to settle down after that huge merger—I think it must have been about a day and a half or so—before I went back to Fred. He is one of the pioneers of cable television and a real visionary too. He suggested that I talk to the folks at Comcast, which was then emerging as a major player in the cable market. Fred thought they'd make a great partner for my project.

I plugged into my network and reached out to my friend Pete Musser, the entrepreneur who'd been one of the earliest investors in cable television before creating Safeguard Scientific. Back in the 1960s Pete had sold a Tupelo, Mississippi, cable television station to another young entrepreneur, Ralph Roberts. The sale marked the beginning of Comcast, now a multi-billion-dollar company. Pete introduced me to Ralph, the founder of Comcast, and that got the ball rolling. Ralph introduced me to Steve Burke, the president and chief operating officer of Comcast, and I pitched him on my vision for Exercise TV!

Time out for a second. Here's an important point for you as a street-smart entrepreneur. When I went to Fred Dressler at Time Warner, he loved my idea but he told me the timing was wrong. Did I get mad? No. Did I quit? No. I stayed in the game! I knew I had a great concept; I just had to wait for the rest of the world to catch up to me. And guess what? It did!

Now there were a lot more twists and turns to the story of how we put the deal together but I'll save them for the next book. For now, understand that at times I felt like I was standing in this big circular room and all around me doors were slamming. This deal was dead at least 700 times. But then it wasn't because I kept trying door after door after door until I found one that opened. You can't give up on the dream because you never know when a door will open. You can't give up because things change so rapidly. One day the timing stinks. The next day, it is perfect.

| *Don't give up on the dream—ever.*

In the end, the deal that is now taking shape for Exercise TV! could be worth as much as a billion dollars some day, with revenues coming from advertising, product sales, and subscriber fees! And it will all have happened because I practice what I preach: I don't quit!

That is the story of this book and the essence of my life as a street-smart entrepreneur. You too will be told *No* time and time again. You too are going to run into dead ends. You will fall on your face. People will lie to you and disappoint you. They'll say they are in when they are not. They'll tell you the deal is done and then tell you it never happened. Remember that success comes when you turn every single *No* into one big *Yes!*

| *Success is failure turned inside out.*

Be ready for it. Be street smart about it. Believe in yourself and in your dreams. And don't let anybody or anything stop you! If you get a little down or things start going sideways, pick up this book again and remind yourself of what it takes to make a street-smart entrepreneur. I promise you that if you keep going, you will succeed. It might not be today or tomorrow, but it will absolutely happen.

You will succeed!

Don't Quit on you!

business by jake power resource guide

Here are the agencies and Web sites I've discussed in the book. Keep this list handy! They offer many services and programs to help the beginning entrepreneur.

Government Agencies

SMALL BUSINESS ADMINISTRATION

The street-smart entrepreneur's best friend! It offers many services including a business matchmaking program and various workshops and tips on starting, expanding, and financing your business.

Every state has at least one local office, listed on their Web site. The national office:

409 3rd Avenue, SW
Washington, D.C. 20416
Tel: 202-205-6770
Web site: www.sba.gov

The SBA's **Investment Division** is also very helpful in providing information on various funding sources and community development grant programs.
Tel: 202-205-6510
Web site: www.sba.gov/INV/

Help for Minority- and Women-Led Businesses

INVESTOR'S CIRCLE

One of the country's oldest and largest investor networks dedicated to nurturing businesses that help society. They especially encourage women-led and minority-owned businesses and concentrate in five specific areas: energy/environment, food/organics, community development, education/media, and health/wellness.

320 Washington Street
Brookline, MA 02445
Tel: 617-566-2600
Web site: www.inbox@investorscircle.net

NATIONAL MINORITY SUPPLIER DEVELOPMENT COUNCIL

A government agency that certifies minority-owned business applying to work with various government agencies.

1040 Avenue of the Americas
Second Floor
New York, New York 10018
Tel: 212-944-2430
Web site: www.nmsdcus.org/

U.S. GENERAL SERVICES ADMINISTRATION (GSA)

GSA's Office of Small Business Utilization advocates for small, minority, veteran, and women business owners.

1800 F Street
Washington, DC 20405
Tel: 202-501-1021
Web site: small.business@gsa.gov

Getting Start-Up Funding

NATIONAL ASSOCIATION OF SMALL BUSINESS INVESTMENT COMPANIES

666 11th Street, NW
Suite 750

Washington, DC 20001
Tel: 202-628-5055
Web site: www.nasbic.org

NATIONAL VENTURE CAPITAL ASSOCIATION
1655 North Ft. Myer Drive
Suite 850
Arlington, VA 22209
Tel: 703-524-2549
Web site: www.nvca.org

ENTREPRENEURIAL MANAGEMENT CENTER
5250 Campanile Drive
San Diego, CA 92182
Tel: 619-594-2781
Web site: www.sdsu.edu/emc

Searching Domain Names and Registering Your Web Site
www.internic.com
www.register.com

Starting Up Non-Profits
The following organizations and Web sites will help you learn about state requirements for nonprofit organizations and help you navigate your way through the maze of philanthropic start-ups:

The Unified Registration Statement (URS)
Web site: www.multistatefiling.org

The Council on Foundations
Web site: www.cof.org

Association of Small Foundations
Web site: www.smallfoundations.org

The Philanthropic Initiative
Web site: wwwtpi.org

The Internet Nonprofit Center
Web site: www.nonprofits.org

The National Council of Nonprofit Associations
Web site: www.ncna.org

Checking Up On Your Personal Credit

You can get your personal credit report by contacting one of the following credit bureaus:

Equifax
Tel: 800-685-1111
Web site: www.equifax.com

Experian
Tel: 888-397-3742
Web site: www. experian.com

TransUnion
Tel: 800-888-4213
Web site: www.transunion.com

index

about the author

Jake Steinfeld, founder and chairman of *Body By Jake* Global LLC is a world-recognized fitness icon and is responsible for creating the personal fitness training industry. In 1993 he launched FitTV, America's first 24-hour fitness lifestyle television network, which he grew to more than 13 million subscribers and sold to FOX Broadcasting just four years later. He is now launching Exercise TV!, a fitness-on-demand network, in partnership with Comcast Corporation. He founded the Don't Quit! Foundation to support and educate adolescents about the value of physical fitness, establishing fitness centers in inner-city middle and high schools. He is also the founder of Major League Lacrosse and author of several previous books including *Get Strong!: Body By Jake's Guide to Building Confidence, Muscles, and a Great Future for Teenage Guys; PowerLiving by Jake: Eleven Lessons to Change Your Life; Don't Quit: Motivation and Exercises to Bring Out the Winner in You;* and *Body By Jake.* He is based in Los Angeles.

the business by jake
live your dream contest

You've read the book! You're fired up! Now I'm going to give you a chance to turn your entrepreneurial dream into reality!

It's simple. All you need to do is tell me about *your* amazing business idea. To get in on the action, go to aol.com/bizbyjake and follow the instructions to enter the contest. Convince me that you have the concept, drive, and *Don't Quit!* attitude you will need to to be a street-smart success and you just might win.

The winner will get $200,000 in cash as seed money to fund his or her dream and a Marquis Jet® card worth $50,000, good for ten hours of flight time on a Citation Ultra. The American Management Association will also send the winner on a five-day, all-expense paid trip to participate in its prestigious *Course for Presidents and CEOs*—a perfect opportunity to rub elbows with successful entrepreneurs and top executives and begin making the kind of contacts that will last a lifetime.

The contest runs through January 31, 2006, so you better get off your buttissimo and get moving!

JAKE